TEACHING
AFRICA
TODAY

*a handbook for teachers and
curriculum planners*

E. JEFFERSON MURPHY,
*Formerly Executive Vice-President,
African-American Institute*

HARRY STEIN,
School Services Division, African-American Institute

Citation Press   New York   1973

For reprint permission, grateful acknowledgment is made to:

Thomas Y. Crowell Company, Inc. for the maps on pp. 65, 70, and 116 from *History of African Civilization* by E. Jefferson Murphy, copyright © 1972 by E. Jefferson Murphy.

Thomas Y. Crowell, Inc. for the map on page 34 from *Understanding Africa* by E. Jefferson Murphy, text copyright © 1969 by E. Jefferson Murphy, illustrations copyright © 1969 by Louise E. Jefferson.

Cover photographs by Louise E. Jefferson

Cover design by Lucy Bitzer

Library of Congress Catalog Card Number: 72-97804
Standard Book Number: 590-09561-7
Printed in the U.S.A.

Acknowledgements

The authors gratefully acknowledge the assistance of the many teachers and supervisors who have offered helpful comments on the structure and approach of this handbook. Special thanks are due Carol Bennett, Richard Bennett, Jane Fitzgerald, Ronald Jubinville, Sister Mary Lyman, Willard Skehan, Shirley Thormann, and Mark Williams for reading chapters or sections and offering detailed criticism, and to Dr. Thomas Weinland of the University of Connecticut School of Education for his very patient reading, commentary, and constructive criticism of the first portions of the book. Merit of the handbook derives in part from their kind cooperation, although the authors alone bear responsibility for any errors or weaknesses.

The support of the Carnegie Corporation of New York, which granted funds to the African-American Institute to defray the costs of writing the handbook as well as for the longer term development of the School Services Program, is also gratefully acknowledged.

Preface

Teaching Africa Today was developed by the School Services Division of the African-American Institute through a grant from the Carnegie Corporation of New York. The book's basic purpose is to assist educators in the preparation of curriculum and to improve the efficiency of their classroom instruction; it is intended for educators involved with students from kindergarten to the twelfth grade.

The African-American Institute is the largest United States private organization working to further African development and to increase American understanding of African economics, culture, and politics and of such issues as human rights and racial equality. It became interested in this project as its School Services Division, through its workshops and other programs, began to identify educator needs in this area.

If there is an overriding generalization to be made about Africa-oriented education, it is that teacher and student interest is outpacing the development of classroom resources and that it is often difficult for teachers to locate those materials that do exist.

We hope this book will serve as a starting point for teachers and curriculum designers. The authors have attempted to define major themes in African studies, suggest a variety of ways in which these themes can be viewed, and provide evaluations of available print and audio-visual resources. Clearly, we hope the book is open-ended enough to provide a ground work upon which teachers can do their own building.

The African-American Institute, in addition to its School Services program, offers a variety of other information services, including a magazine—*Africa Report*—African travel and study opportunities for American educators and students, seminars and conferences, and the dissemination of information on current issues in United States-African relations.

In its development work, AAI—since its founding in 1953—has administered scholarship programs that have provided more than 3,000 Africans with higher education in the United States. In recent years, the Institute's development thrust has broadened to include the problems of rural change in Africa and work in nonformal or out-of-school education programs.

As president of AAI, I tend to view all our work as either touching on or directly involving education. As I have talked with educators around the United States, I have become convinced that African studies hold a potential for discovery that few other disciplines can match. The study of Africa offers not only insight into other cultures but lets us look at our own culture in a new light, particularly with reference to problems in race relations—perhaps the most important problems we in America now face. Americans have much to learn from Africa, and I hope this book will be useful to both you and your students as you tackle these complex subjects.

William R. Cotter

PRESIDENT

AFRICAN-AMERICAN INSTITUTE

NEW YORK CITY

Contents

2 African History I: From Human Origins to the Period of European Influence 61

3 African History II: Developments during the Contact with Europe 84

Introduction: on teaching about Africa

There are two major characteristics of this handbook that make it somewhat different from other books available to those who are teaching about Africa.

First, each chapter is a very condensed commentary on the subject it covers. Each sets forth the most important principles, features, themes, problems, concepts, or issues that characterize its subject. The chapter on African geography, for example, is devoted to the essential features of African geography: those aspects and concepts which the student ought to grasp if he is to gain a basic understanding of man and land in Africa. It does not summarize *all* the details of climate, landforms, water systems, topography, products, and ecology that would be required for a comprehensive geographic survey. An entire book would be needed to do this. There are already available several good books and chapters in books that will provide the teacher with the necessary details. These books and other teacher aids are listed at the end of the geography chapter.

Similarly, the chapters on history concentrate on major themes and forces that have characterized and shaped African history. Although very condensed chronologies are provided in outline form for easy reference, the teacher is referred to the recommended books and other materials listed in the section following the two history chapters. In these materials, which have been carefully selected and clearly annotated, will she find the detailed treatments the chronological outlines merely suggest.

The second feature of this handbook is that materials are given heavy emphasis. Each chapter or, in two cases pairs of chapters on related subjects, is followed by a list of books, films, maps, slides, tapes, charts, and other materials. These materials are grouped into Teacher Reference and Classroom Use categories. Each recommended item is identified, described, annotated, and evaluated, its source is indicated, and its price, when available, is noted.

In addition, Chapter Nine is devoted to a discussion of how to select, evaluate, and use materials. This information is especially important since new materials are constantly appearing and old ones are becoming obsolete or difficult to obtain. The Appendix lists most of the sources of materials and information on Africa, with current addresses.

The teacher who has recently surveyed materials on Africa will recognize immediately the crucial importance of this emphasis on materials and the materials lists. There are countless kinds of materials now available, ranging from inexpensive to costly, short to long, and excellent to deplorable. Only an expert, with unlimited time, can make a reliable appraisal and selection from this great variety. The staff of the School Services Division of the African-American Institute, educators with extensive experience in African and American schools have spent years collecting and evaluating materials on Africa as well as discussing with teachers their utility in the classroom. The lists in this handbook represent their authoritative judgments on what are most reliable and useful.

The style of this handbook is deliberately succinct and practical. It recognizes that most teachers do not have the time to undertake an exhaustive study of Africa before entering the classroom and that most will have neither visited Africa nor studied it extensively before teaching about it. It assumes that the average teacher wants a brief, simply presented guide to African studies that reflects the best judgment of scholars and educators who have specialized in this area and who are familiar with the needs of the classroom teacher and her students.

How to Use the Handbook

First, you should read the Introduction carefully, regardless of the level at which you will be teaching and the approach you may plan to use in the classroom. It is designed to help you define your objectives, to be conscious of the reasons why Africa is studied, to identify the strategy you will follow, and to be alert for the pitfalls you may encounter in many textbooks or other materials.

The handbook is written primarily for teachers who are responsible for African study between grades five and twelve. Surveys of national trends have shown that these are the grades in which Africa is most frequently studied. Teachers who are teaching about Africa in lower elementary grades, however, will find much of the book useful as well; the chapter on African geography is specifically planned for use at any grade level.

Second, taking into account the grade level, the number of weeks you have available, the needs of your students, and the broader curriculum within which you will treat Africa, skim through the chapters that deal with the areas you believe you should cover. For this purpose, an intensive reading is unnecessary. Each chapter highlights its material with subheads so that you can quickly gain an overview of its scope and emphases.

Third, select those chapters you find relevant to your needs and read them more carefully. Each is short enough to be read within an hour or two. Then look carefully at the materials listed at the end of the chapter to select those you wish to review, either for your own reference or for classroom use. A perusal of Chapter Nine will also be helpful at this point.

Fourth, make an outline of your lesson plans, noting the films, slides, maps, and other audio-visuals you may wish to use at various stages. The handbook does not provide lesson plans; most teachers prefer to construct their own or to follow those contained in textbooks or curriculum guides. Teachers who follow structured approaches will find that the chapters of the handbook are organized in such a way that their sections can be used as a rough guide to the construction of lesson plans. Teachers who are committed to inquiry teaching will find that the concepts, forces, and questions that appear frequently in each chapter can be used as foci for planning inquiry sequences.

You will find that this process will enable you to plan out a surprisingly complete approach even before you go beyond the handbook to read more detailed treatments of the subjects you will teach. If you are familiar with the subject from previous study or teaching experience, you may find that your preparation is sufficient. If you are unfamiliar with Africa, or if you plan to devote a number of weeks to intensive study of various aspects, you will, of course, find that the handbook has not prepared you fully or supplied you with all the data you need. At this point you will find the lists of materials invaluable in helping you select those items you wish to consult for your own preparation and for use in the classroom.

Strategies, Objectives, and Approaches

In many cases a school or school system includes a study of Africa in the curriculum to satisfy objectives over which an individual teacher may have no control. In other cases the teacher may have considerable freedom in structuring the strategy and objectives, and the school administration may look to her for leadership and initiative. Whichever the case, a teacher should be well versed in the reasons why Africa is worth studying, in the kinds of objectives that may be met, and in the several strategies that may be used to attain these objectives.

There are six broad reasons usually adduced for including Africa in the curriculum. They are not mutually exclusive, and similar approaches may be used in several. Yet each reason does imply a particular strategy and a set of objectives. Each also suggests a certain pattern of subjects and priorities. A teacher cannot prepare an effective lesson plan unless she understands clearly the curricular reason or reasons why her school is including a study of Africa and the broad objectives that study is expected to achieve.

First, Africa may be studied because it is the ancestral home of roughly one American in eight. This is sometimes called the *African Heritage* approach. Both Afro-Americans and Americans of different ethnic origin are increasingly interested in a better understanding of the history of the Afro-

American and his African heritage. Increasingly, contemporary issues in Africa evoke more Afro-American interest in modern Africa, just as the problems of Ireland and Israel compel attention by Irish and Jewish Americans. Belatedly Americans are recognizing that the Afro-American has played an important and contributory role in building America; now the evidence is accumulating that the African has played a constructive role in the shaping of Western civilization.

Second, Africa may be studied simply because it is a part of the world. This is sometimes called the *World Study* approach. No American citizen of the future can function with full effectiveness unless he has some understanding of *all* the world, past and present. If a student is studying world history, he must pay some attention to African history; if he is studying world geography, African geography must be included.

Third, Africa may be studied as a part of a broader study of the non-Western world of Asia, Africa, the Middle East, and Latin America. This is usually called the *non-Western Studies* focus. Africa, Asia, Latin America, and the Middle East were conspicuously neglected in the American curriculum until after World War II. Many educators, as well as a significant segment of the American public, argue plausibly that this neglect must be corrected. They hold that no American can be considered educated if he is largely ignorant of the lands and people that constitute some two thirds of humanity.

Fourth, Africa's peoples may be studied, emphasizing their cultures, languages, arts, and traditional economies. This is usually called the *Peoples and Cultures* approach. It is distinctively anthropological in spirit, even though it may be carried out in either elementary school or higher grades. It rests on the belief that a well-educated person can gain a better understanding of human nature and the ways of society if he studies man in many areas, living under many conditions.

Fifth, Africa's contemporary problems and tensions may be studied. This approach is called by many names: *World Problems*, *Current Issues*, and others. Many educators believe that education, especially in high school, is enhanced by leading students through the process of examining problems and issues, helping to develop qualities of critical thinking and objectivity. Thus a student acquires a better understanding of problems that face his society and the world, so that he can fulfill his citizenship responsibilities more ably. Africa abounds with important problems: apartheid and racial oppression in Southern Africa, economic underdevelopment, colonialism and neocolonialism, human freedoms, disease eradication, education, and nation building.

Sixth, Africa may be studied for its own sake, because it is important and has been traditionally neglected in the curriculum. As a major producer of dozens of strategic minerals and vegetable products, Africa has considerable importance in the world economy. In the United Nations its countries form the largest bloc of any world region. It attracts American attention because, after so long being unknown, it seems suddenly to have emerged into prominence. This approach is generally called the *African Study* or *African Survey* approach.

Although the movement to add African study to the curriculum continues to expand and there is general public assent to it, there is no widespread consensus on any one of these six broad reasons for adding it. The reason for studying Africa, and the approach used, vary from region to region, state to state, and frequently from school to school or teacher to teacher. Some of the approaches have a controversial quality. The first, for example, tends to arouse strong partisanship among Black Americans and some liberal Whites. Some conservative thinkers, including a minority of Afro-Americans, regard it with reservation; they fear that it may weaken Afro-American loyalties to America or increase racial tensions Some people take issue with the sixth; they argue that Africa is not really very important to America and that there are far more pressing needs that should be addressed by the curriculum.

Some teachers will be in the position of having to teach a course on Africa with the rationale and approach already set by the school, the district, or the state. For her a knowledge of alternative approaches may help her plan and conduct her course more confidently. Other teachers will have great freedom to choose the approach, and they may be called upon to defend both their approach and the inclusion of Africa in the curriculum. In either case, they should be clear, when planning the course, on the rationale and approach.

Problems in Planning the Course

Once a teacher has clarified the rationale and approach, she faces several more complex problems—most of which are either avoided in many textbooks or are decided arbitrarily. These problems group naturally into four categories: first, whether to study all of Africa, Africa south of the Sahara only, or only one or two countries; second, how to strike some balance between the many commonalities and diversities of Africa; third, identifying and trying to overcome the many myths and stereotypes Americans hold about Africa, which severely impede real understanding; and fourth, recognizing and dealing with a common tendency to oversimplify African matters to make them fit American patterns of thinking more comfortably.

These four problem groups warrant further examination.

First, most available textbooks and materials currently used in schools tend to treat Africa south of the Sahara as a unit, separating northern Africa for study within the Middle Eastern area. Most Africans take sharp exception to this concept, as do most American scholars who specialize in African studies. A formidable idea in modern African political thought is that of African unity. Politically conscious Africans regard the entire continent as one Africa and regard the Western tendency to dichotomize between the regions north and south of the Sahara as an effort to disunify Africans. Without equivocation this handbook recommends the inclusion of *all* of Africa in any course of African studies.

This is not to ignore the differences in history, racial mixture, religion, and culture that do indeed delineate Africa into regions. Africa is not a homogeneous whole. The Sahara has acted as an impediment to the free interplay of ideas and peoples between north and south. But the Sahara has also served, like a sea, as a bridge, and one can easily exaggerate the differences between the peoples to its north and south.

On purely educational grounds there is a growing tendency among educators to oppose the study of Africa as a whole, on the more reasonable ground that it is too large, too populous, and too subdivided into distinct countries to be understood as one unit. These educators argue that students should concentrate on one country or at most a region of three or four countries.

The authors of this handbook accept the educational soundness of this point of view. They recommend that a teacher focus on one country or one region for intensive study and illustration but that some time be devoted to sketching out the broad features of Africa as a whole. Africa is a real concept; it is an entity in more than a purely geographic sense. Hundreds of millions of people regard themselves as Africans. The student must not, therefore, ignore this reality by spending all his time on one country or one people. There must be some compromise between the reality of Africa as a unit and the sound educational principle of focusing on a smaller, more manageable, unit for concentrated study.

Second, there has long been great controversy over the extent of homogeneity and diversity within Africa. One school of thought treats Africa as though it were one large homogeneous area, with one culture and one people. An opposing school of thought argues that Africa is fundamentally heterogeneous, pointing to its more than 800 languages and tribes, its variety of races, its nearly fifty countries, its diversity of traditional cultures, and the tensions and antagonisms that seem characteristics of this diversity.

This problem is both political and factual in nature. In fact Africa is, of course, a continent of diversity, but it possesses numerous commonalities as well. Politically, however, Africans and many of their friends abroad prefer to stress the commonalities, because they believe, with some justification, that there has long been a Western tendency to emphasize Africa's heterogeneity in order to divide its peoples against each other. African thinkers argue that there are deep bonds of similarity in world view, in social structure, in ideologies, and in attitudes about life that bind all Africans together despite other differences.

This handbook recommends strongly that the teacher steer a carefully objective course in this area. Throughout the handbook an effort has been made to adhere to this objective position; both commonalities and variations are noted consistently in each chapter wherever it is appropriate.

The third problem is perhaps the most difficult of all. It has become widely recognized that Americans and Europeans have long held views of Africa that are distorted by myths and stereotypes. These myths and stereotypes are centuries old, dating back to the era of the slave trade. They color many of our modern perceptions of Africans and their countries. But they are often deeply buried; most of us are not aware we hold them. Because of their unconscious nature, they often creep into otherwise convincing textbooks and materials by reputable educational publishers, newspapers, and the electronic media.

In recent years our expanding knowledge of Africa has helped to explode some of the most obvious of these myths. Generally it is known that there are no tigers in Africa; that most wild game is concentrated in carefully tended game parks; that most of the continent is dry, rather than jungle-like; that Africa does have periods of glory in its history; that there are cities and modern amenities in some parts of the continent; that some Africans have received a high standard of education and have distinguished themselves in the intellectual and international arenas. We no longer wear Tarzan's spectacles in our perceptions of Africa.

Yet the stereotypes that produced these myths about

Africa and its people still remain. We still see Africans living in "tribes," making little or no distinction between the populous, highly cultured, and affluent Ashanti nation and the small bands of Khoisan peoples, denigratingly called Bushmen by Europeans who roam the Kalahari Desert. We still think of Africa as so underdeveloped that we find it difficult to visualize the many thousands of miles of railroad and paved highways or the numerous modern airports that are actually quite common. We still view Africans as ridden by superstition and vast ignorance. We still imagine the average African to be somewhat bewildered by modernity and conscious of his tribal identity but largely ignorant of his national identity.

All these stereotypes, and many more, remain in our minds because our ancestors depicted the African as something less than human in order to try to avoid the moral dilemma that the slave trade aroused. Although our more recent ancestors should have known better, the old stereotypes were expanded and strengthened in the late nineteenth century in an effort to justify the European conquest and colonial partition of Africa. These stereotypes have begun to weaken only since the late 1950s, when Africans began to enter the modern world as their own spokesmen and large numbers of foreign visitors began to go to Africa and discovered that many of their previous perceptions were erroneous.

This is not the place to undertake a listing and refutation of the surviving myths and stereotypes. The handbook is, in a sense, devoted to this essential task. Each chapter helps the teacher identify and dispel myths by emphasizing the reality. The materials lists deliberately omit badly biased and distorted films, books, supplements, and other materials.

When materials with bias are listed, their biases are described; often a bad film is as effective in showing students how we unconsciously distort our views of Africa as one that is produced for that purpose.

To illustrate this, consider three brief examples.

In the study of African geography, many materials portray equatorial Africa as a hot, humid, dank, and unpleasant region, relatively sparsely populated by people whose energy level is low and whose agricultural productivity is inadequate. This characterization is based more on stereotype than on reality. The rain forests of western Africa are the most densely populated large regions of the continent; the people who live there are among Africa's wealthiest and most progressive; temperatures are usually tempered by altitude, ocean breezes, or a high evaporation rate. (Many an African from Lagos, Accra, or Abidjan, while sweltering in the summer heat of Washington, D.C., or New York, has expressed a fervent desire to be back in his own home where such extremes are unknown.)

Nor is it generally pointed out, when discussing African climates, that modern geographers are far from unanimous in concluding that climate has the direct effect on human behavior and energy levels that was once believed. This is especially true in tropical Africa, where men in some of the warmer and more humid regions are among the most energetic on the continent. Tropical climates have indeed been responsible for lowering energy levels, but indirectly, by providing good breeding conditions for bacteria and insects that cause vitality-sapping diseases: malaria, bilharzia, dysentery, and the like. Once these diseases are controlled, as they have been in parts of Africa, people become more energetic.

A second case in point is that of religion. We commonly characterize African religious beliefs as pagan, animist, primitive, or crude. African religious activities are generally grouped under such categories as witchcraft, sorcery, magic, ju-ju, ancestor worship, or spirit worship.

The fact is that virtually every African religion is based on a belief in a God who is conceived as the creator of man and the universe. Thus Africans are monotheistic. Their belief in God differs from that of Judaism, Christianity, and Islam, of course, because Africans widely regard God as being somewhat remote from the affairs of men; they believe He has appointed spirits (not a very different concept from that of angels or saints) to act as intermediaries between Him and living man. Man thus offers gifts and sacrifices to the spirits of his ancestors or of certain natural phenomena, because he believes that this is God's design.

Where African religions have been carefully studied, they have been found to be complex and extensive. Their internal logic is generally as consistent as that of the great religions of Western man, if one accepts the basic premises about God and nature. Many Africans prefer to adhere to their traditional religions, even when they have had close contact with Islam or Christianity. Witchcraft and magic, which admittedly still exist in Africa, persist mainly in groups where scientific causality is unknown, because disease and misfortune require explanations. Both, however, have declined rapidly where scientific knowledge has gained a foothold, and neither is an essential part of deeper African religious beliefs.

The third example is our tendency to think of the African as a person living in primitive conditions within tribal societies. This image is so strongly entrenched that some teachers have reported difficulty in interesting their students in the study of Africans who are educated, live in cities, and who dress in modern clothes. The Nigerian businessman driving to work in his Fiat or Peugeot, neatly dressed in a suit with a tie, after having brushed his teeth with Colgate or Crest, is regarded as somehow un-African. We continue to imagine that the "real" African must be totally different from anything we know and must conform to the age-old image of a tribalized peasant. Despite the fact that there are very few such Africans left (there were never as many as our stereotype assumed), we continue to regard the changing African, who is nowadays the real African, as somehow an exception.

The teacher is urged to pay special attention to the many myths and stereotypes this handbook will identify; true understanding of Africa is impossible unless they are exposed and dispelled.

The fourth problem in planning an African study, that of oversimplification, is related to the third. It is the natural tendency to categorize and simplify complex phenomena to make them fit intelligibly into our existing knowledge structure. Both journalists and textbook writers find it difficult to resist oversimplification; they have an obligation to state facts in terms that are readily understandable to their readers. The more distant and poorly known the phenomenon, the greater the tendency to oversimplify. Much of the present lack of understanding about Africa is as due to oversimplification as to myth and stereotype.

Two examples will illustrate this crucial problem.

First, Africa is frequently characterized as being "in ferment." The image conjured up is that of social disorder, instability in everyday life, and widespread confusion. Nothing could be farther from the truth.

The man on the street in Africa deems himself generally

safer and more secure than he imagines the average American to be. Many African visitors to the United States arrive here with deep apprehensions about muggings, civil disorder, robbery, and conflict. In his homeland there may be an occasional *coup d'état* but rarely any civil disorder or molestation of the average person. Governmental changes are generally quiet and without bloodshed.

Daily life in most of Africa centers around familiar problems: how to make ends meet, how to get the children through school, how to obtain better housing or better clothes, and other similar problems that affect all people. The tenor of life is generally more relaxed than in the United States; people are sociable and leisurely even though many are hard workers. There is rarely any perception of "ferment."

Second, Africa is widely thought of as a "tribal" land, in which people are sharply divided into closely knit tribal groups that command their loyalties and shape their behavior. When conflicts have erupted in African countries (a familiar case being the Nigerian civil war when Biafra attempted to secede), it is a common tendency in America to see them as "tribal" conflicts. And the newspapers and television reports do describe them as such.

In fact, most Africans have surprisingly little tribal feeling, and little of their behavior stems from their ethnic origin or affiliation. As noted earlier, African traditional societies range in size from tiny autonomous bands of less than one hundred people up to great nations of millions of people. Most Africans, like Americans, have multiple identities: as father, husband, farmer, church member, member of a fraternal society or guild, member of a clan or extended family, member of a loosely knit ethnic group, and as a member of a national state. Africans find these plural identities no more contradictory or confusing than other human beings, except when forceful problems of an economic or political nature intervene. In this respect the African is in no way different from individuals in any other part of the world. In case of conflict an individual will act on the basis of a deeply ingrained priority of his many identities, but ethnic affiliation is not necessarily the highest priority identity in most Africans.

In the Nigerian conflict, ethnic identity was called into prominence by the political leaders when other forces (control of federal agencies, shares of oil revenues, access to skilled jobs, political rivalry for power) produced a secessionist movement. Yet many Ibos remained at work in federal areas, some in high government positions; others who supported secession did so with grave doubts and reluctance. With the federal military victory, most Ibos quickly regained their identity as Nigerians, and their identity as Biafrans was speedily weakened, if not forgotten.

Americans generally analyzed the Nigerian tragedy quite incorrectly. The major reason for the faulty analysis was the tendency to see the conflict in terms of tribal conflict. Almost all the best newspapers, magazines, radio, and television reports constantly reiterated the "tribal" roots of the conflict. The Ibo and Hausa were ubiquitously described as traditional enemies, as though this explained why the war began. Not only are the Hausa and Ibo *not* traditional enemies (they had very minimal contact prior to the twentieth century), but the focus on this alleged enmity obscured many more important factors. The constant emphasis on "tribal" tensions served to reaffirm our deeply buried stereotype of the African as a primitive being, automatically thinking of himself as a member of a "tribe" rather than of a nation.

Teachers will find frequent emphasis on these points throughout the handbook. While a certain degree of generalization and simplification are essential to learning, the teacher must help students avoid the extremes that lead to a distorted view of past and present African affairs.

Suggestions from Africans

In an effort to obtain African views about what Americans should consider teaching about Africa, the School Services Division of the African-American Institute prepared a questionnaire in 1969 that was sent to over six hundred Africans in the United States and in Africa. Nearly two hundred replies were received. Slightly over half were from West Africans, and twenty percent were from both East Africans and Southern Africans. Less than five percent of the responses came from North Africans.

American educators might find it useful to consider these viewpoints expressed by these Africans before they design new lessons or units:

☐ Stereotypes should be avoided at all costs. These often fall into the following categories:

Geographic. Very few areas of the continent can be characterized as tropical rain forest or "jungle." Most of the continent is a plateau, with vast expanses of open grasslands or areas of mixed trees and grasslands. Africa consists of a wide range of topographic and climatic regions.

Terminology. Educators should stress the existence of the

more than forty independent states in Africa, which are inhabited by peoples who differ physically, culturally, and linguistically. Students should be cautioned to distinguish between different areas and their diverse problems. Vague, inclusive generalizations and the expedient use of the collective term "Africa" to describe a vast continent with over 340 million inhabitants must be avoided.

Cultural bias. African peoples, known to Europeans as Bushmen, Hottentots, and Pygmies, do not call themselves by such terms. These words represent denigrations applied to African peoples by Europeans. Bushmen-Hottentot peoples call themselves Khoi-Khoi or Khoisan peoples. The word "pygmy" is Greek. Neighboring Africans call these peoples Mbuti or Binga.

Economic. More attention should be given to African urban areas, industrial developments and tourism. While agriculture, both subsistence and monetary is still the source of sustenance for eighty to eighty-five percent of Africa's peoples, other economic sectors are growing rapidly.

☐ Nearly all respondents pleaded for an understanding of African *cultural values.* The need for teachers to develop an eclectic and transcultural student outlook is identical to that of American educators working in Asian or Latin American studies. African forms of expression, institutions of marriage, organization of family, and religious beliefs all meet African needs and aspirations. They reflect, in their own ways, the responses of specific human societies to universal needs for social organization and social controls. Africans identify with the land, natural forces within nature, and the supernatural. Although there are exceptions, these feelings are very strong throughout the continent. Curriculum units that deal with

African religions and value systems are needed. African literature may prove helpful in achieving such insights.

☐ There was a wide variety of opinion concerning the choice of subjects through which to investigate Africa. The geographical approach, encompassing physical, cultural, and economic aspects, was favored. Many respondents also felt that some historical background was essential. The majority stated that the focus should be on *contemporary Africa* and Africans. Some felt that a core or cross-disciplinary approach was needed, in which traditional history and geography would be combined with literature, sociology, economics, and political science. Emphasis upon current urban developments, religion and ethics, and problems of modernization were also mentioned.

☐ Nearly all respondents believed that North Africa should *not* be treated separately from the remainder of Africa. The entire continent should be taught as a unit; however, North Africa could also be taught in conjunction with Southwest Asian or Mediterranean studies. Many respondents revealed a Pan-Africanistic attitude in this regard, stating that recent European colonialism had unnaturally divided the peoples and states of the continent.

European ignorance of Africa's early history overlooked the importance of the long record of cultural and economic contacts between Africans north and south of the Sahara. The peoples of Northern Africa are in some ways unlike those in other parts of the continent, but their basic contemporary economic and political status, as well as their recent colonial history, bind them closely to other Africans. Studies of Africa and African culture should include North African examples. Educators should avoid the development of such courses as sub-Saharan or tropical or Black Africa, which exclude North Africa. These are arbitrary geographical definitions, created by non-Africans, that do an injustice to the African reality.

☐ Southern Africa is the most neglected region of the continent in the American curriculum. The forty-two Southern Africans who answered the questionnaire stressed the need to acquaint Americans with the region and its problems. Many noted similarities between the efforts of non-Whites in the United States and those in Southern Africa to effect beneficial change. American interests and official United States government foreign policy in the area should also be emphasized in any assessment of the area.

In summary, an analysis of the returned questionnaires stresses the following ideas:

☐ Beware of stereotypes and myths
☐ Stress contemporary Africa, with historical background
☐ Focus on the humans of the continent, rather than just physical or economic geography
☐ Recognize the vast diversity within the continent
☐ Mix rural and traditional studies with both urban and modern sectors
☐ Include North Africa
☐ Stress Southern Africa
☐ Link Africa to other continents of the world with similar problems and recent historical backgrounds. This will allow comparisons and integrate Africa into a worldwide perspective.

There are probably African students studying in colleges and universities near your school. They can be easily contacted through the Foreign Student Advisor or the Registrar's Office. Their viewpoints may be useful in developing curriculum and selecting materials. Many institutions of higher education have African faculty members who can also be involved in the planning process.

Planning an African Course

This section offers suggestions, and suggestions only, to those teachers who may have had no previous experience teaching Africa in the classroom or who are redesigning a previously offered course. It is not intended as a prescribed curriculum or course outline to be rigidly followed, but it does suggest the subjects recommended by the authors for inclusion in each of the major approaches described on pages 5 through 8. (The *World Study* approach has been subdivided into World or Regional History and World or Regional Geography, and a seventh approach, *International Relations*, has been added. The latter is added because occasional courses with this approach are offered in the upper grades of high school.)

The course plans outlined here offer suggestions for what subjects to emphasize and what proportional emphasis they might be given, depending on the approach or strategy and the length of time available for the African course. Using the eight chapters of the handbook as units, the suggested course outlines are organized according to the number of weeks available for the entire course. Depending upon the time available, each course outline then suggests the amount of time, in days of one class period each, which the teacher may wish to spend on each of the units recommended for inclusion in the study program. Should the school schedule not allow five days per week, proportional reductions can be made as follows: for a four-period week, multiply the recommended days by 0.8; for a three-period week, multiply by 0.6. Thus, if the recommended program suggests five days for geography, four days would be used in a four-period week and three days in a three-period week.

Where the number of weeks available is different, the teacher can extrapolate from the recommended programs; if six weeks were suggested, the program could be constructed by extrapolating between the recommended programs for four and eight weeks, for example. In the rare situations where two semesters are available, the teacher may double the suggested times for the sixteen-week program she is using.

Unit One:	African Geography (Chapter One)
Unit Two:	African History I (Chapter Two)
Unit Three:	African History II (Chapter Three)
Unit Four:	Building African Nations I (Chapter Four)
Unit Five:	Building African Nations II (Chapter Five)
Unit Six:	Africa and the World (Chapter Six)
Unit Seven:	Africa and America (Chapter Seven)
Unit Eight:	Southern Africa (Chapter Eight)

SUGGESTED COURSE OUTLINES

African Heritage

FOUR-WEEK PROGRAM		EIGHT-WEEK PROGRAM	
Unit One	4–5 days	Unit One	4–5 days
Unit Two	8–9 days	Unit Two	10–15 days
Unit Three	8–9 days	Unit Three	10–15 days
		Unit Seven	5–10 days

African Heritage

TWELVE-WEEK PROGRAM

Unit One	4–5 days
Unit Two	10–15 days
Unit Three	10–15 days
Unit Five	10–15 days

or

Unit Eight	10–15 days
Unit Seven	5–10 days

SIXTEEN-WEEK PROGRAM

Unit One	5 days
Unit Two	15 days
Unit Three	15 days
Unit Four	10 days
Unit Five	15 days
Unit Seven	10 days
Unit Eight	10 days

Non-Western Studies

FOUR-WEEK PROGRAM

Unit One	5 days
Unit Two	5 days
Unit Three	5 days
Unit Four	5 days

EIGHT-WEEK PROGRAM

Unit One	5 days
Unit Two	5 days
Unit Three	10 days
Unit Four	10 days
Unit Five	10 days

TWELVE-WEEK PROGRAM

Unit One	5 days
Unit Two	10 days
Unit Three	10 days
Unit Four	15 days
Unit Five	10 days
Unit Six	10 days

SIXTEEN-WEEK PROGRAM

Unit One	5 days
Unit Two	10 days
Unit Three	10 days
Unit Four	15 days
Unit Five	15 days
Unit Six	10 days
Unit Seven	15 days

or

Unit Eight	15 days

World or Regional History

FOUR-WEEK PROGRAM

Unit Two	10 days
Unit Three	10 days

EIGHT-WEEK UNIT

Unit One	3 days
Unit Two	17 days
Unit Three	20 days

TWELVE-WEEK UNIT

Unit One	5 days
Unit Two	20 days
Unit Three	20 days

TWELVE-WEEK UNIT

Unit Four   15 days

SIXTEEN-WEEK UNIT

Unit One   5 days
Unit Two   25 days
Unit Three   25 days
Unit Four   15 days
Unit Five   10 days

World or Regional Geography
(Assumes no more than
twelve weeks)

FOUR-WEEK PROGRAM

Unit One   20 days

EIGHT-WEEK PROGRAM

Unit One   30 days
Unit Four   10 days

TWELVE-WEEK PROGRAM

Unit One   40 days
Unit Four   20 days

Peoples and Cultures
(Assumes no more than
twelve weeks)

FOUR-WEEK PROGRAM

Unit One   5 days
Unit Two   15 days

EIGHT-WEEK PROGRAM

Unit One   5 days
Unit Two   20 days

Unit Five   15 days

TWELVE-WEEK PROGRAM

Unit One   5 days
Unit Two   20 days
Unit Four   15 days
Unit Five   20 days

Current Issues
(Assumes no more
than twelve weeks)

FOUR-WEEK PROGRAM

Unit Four   5 days
Unit Five   5 days
Unit Six   5 days
Unit Seven   5 days
               or
Unit Eight   5 days

EIGHT-WEEK PROGRAM

Unit Four   5 days
Unit Five   5 days
Unit Six   10 days
Unit Seven   10 days
Unit Eight   10 days

TWELVE-WEEK PROGRAM

Unit Four   10 days
Unit Five   10 days
Unit Six   10 days
Unit Seven   15 days
Unit Eight   15 days

Africa Survey

FOUR-WEEK PROGRAM

Unit One	3 days
Unit Two	4 days
Unit Three	3 days
Unit Four	5 days
Unit Six	5 days

EIGHT-WEEK PROGRAM

Unit One	5 days
Unit Two	5 days
Unit Three	5 days
Unit Four	10 days
Unit Five	10 days
Unit Six	5 days

TWELVE-WEEK PROGRAM

Unit One	5 days
Unit Two	5 days
Unit Three	10 days
Unit Four	10 days
Unit Five	10 days
Unit Six	10 days
Unit Eight	10 days

SIXTEEN-WEEK PROGRAM

Unit One	5 days
Unit Two	10 days
Unit Three	10 days
Unit Four	15 days
Unit Five	15 days
Unit Six	10 days
Unit Seven	5 days
Unit Eight	10 days

International Relations
(Assumes no more
than twelve weeks)

FOUR-WEEK PROGRAM

Unit Four	5 days
Unit Six	5 days
Unit Seven	5 days
Unit Eight	5 days

EIGHT-WEEK PROGRAM

Unit Four	5 days
Unit Five	5 days
Unit Six	10 days
Unit Seven	10 days
Unit Eight	10 days

TWELVE-WEEK PROGRAM

Unit Four	10 days
Unit Five	5 days
Unit Six	15 days
Unit Seven	15 days
Unit Eight	15 days

SEQUENCE

The handbook follows a traditional sequence, beginning with geography and moving chronologically through history to contemporary Africa. This is emphatically *not* meant to suggest that teachers must follow the same sequence in the classroom. Many teachers will prefer to begin with a study of modern African social life or problems of nation building, leaving geography and history for later study.

In inquiry teaching, especially, a traditional sequence may be inappropriate. Most teachers who use the inquiry method have found that the inquiry process is best initiated by helping students to focus on questions that have direct relevance to their own experience or that pose challenging questions of an ethical or value nature.

When the teacher begins to plan her lessons, she will have to make decisions about the sequence that seems most compatible with her teaching style and her experience with the kinds of students she will be working with. A good teacher whose approach is traditional may find it logical to follow the sequence used by the handbook, but other equally good teachers may rearrange the sequence radically. This is a matter best left up to the individual teacher.

The sequence used in preparing the handbook was convenient for the authors, but that convenience is its only justification. No teacher should feel constrained to follow it unless it accords with her own style and experience.

1 *African geography: man and land*

Most teachers are fully aware of the numbing effects an incorrect approach to teaching geography can have. Virtually all students are bored by seemingly endless presentations of climatic features, landforms, soil types, vegetation zones, crops, minerals, rivers, mountains, lakes, and elevations. When geography is thus presented, students normally emerge with little real understanding of how man uses his natural environment or how that environment has continually presented its inhabitants with challenges, problems, and opportunities.

The producers of many textbooks and classroom materials still seem to find it difficult to devise more interesting and effective approaches. That task is too often left to the teacher. And when the teacher is working under a heavy teaching schedule, with little time for research and experimentation, the task is especially difficult.

Teaching African geography is a chronic problem, partly because good materials have only recently become available and partly because most teachers, like most Americans, have had little knowledge of or experience with African geography themselves. The little they studied in high school or college is frequently inaccurate and misleading. Futhermore, too little was known of African geography twenty or thirty years ago to insure good materials and courses.

The outline that follows has been carefully selected in an effort to cull out unnecessary details, so that the teacher can concentrate on those features of African geography that have a significant influence on the ways Africans have lived in history, on their contemporary lives, or on their plans for the future.

Careful thought has also been given to organizing these salient features in a way that can be most directly and effectively utilized by the teacher, beginning with simple and critical features, then moving on to more complex ones.

In every section there are suggestions for techniques of presentation and explanation that will help the teacher make the material most relevant and understandable to students, usually through the use of map comparisons, references to figures, or analogies with concepts and phenomena that American students are likely to be familiar with. It is important to note that no effort has been made to present a complete, step-by-step "mini-course" on African geography, which would allow the teacher no freedom in presentation and illustration. Most teachers have their own favored methods and techniques and are constrained, rather than assisted, by overly detailed teaching guides.

The materials below present a reasonably complete outline of African geography that can be covered in as little as three class periods; they are sufficient, however, for considerably more than this if time is available and if a teacher wishes to utilize discussion techniques or student projects. The films, slides, maps, and other materials recommended at the end of this chapter will prove useful to the class that devotes more than three periods to African geography.

OUTLINE:
Characteristics of the African Environment

A. Africa is a huge continent
   1. World's second largest, after Asia.
   2. Area: 11,732,717 square miles.

   Comparison. Africa is nearly *four* times the size of the United States (3,022,387 sq. miles) excluding Alaska, and over *three* times the size of the United States including Alaska (3,593,387 sq. miles).

   Illustration. Show students the map of Africa with the United States superimposed on it. Place cutouts of two U.S. states (your own state plus Texas, 267,339 sq. miles) on the same-scale map of Africa. Note that even Texas, legendary for its large size, appears tiny. Compare Texas with several African nations, both with the cutouts and square mile comparisons: Republic of Sudan (977,499); Zaire (formerly Congo) (904,991); Republic of South Africa (472,359); Tanzania (363,708).

B. Africa's size is important
   1. Low population density: less than 350,000,000 people, or 30 persons per square mile.

   Comparison. United States population is more than 200,000,000, or nearly 70 persons per square mile. Population of United Kingdom is approximately 53,000,000 in an area of 93,895 sq. miles, or roughly 560 persons per square mile.

   2. Distances are great: Cape Town to Cairo nearly 5,000 miles; Somalia to Senegal nearly 5,000 miles. Within most countries distances are great, making it difficult to maintain communications between

major cities and isolated rural areas and between the coast (where most African capitals are located) and the interior. Within Nigeria one may have to travel 1,000 miles to reach the capital, Lagos; within Tanzania, more than 800 miles to reach the capital, Dar es Salaam; within Algeria, more than 1,000 miles to reach Algiers; 1,000 miles from Cape Town to Johannesburg.

3. With such great distances, the cost of building highways and railroads is great, especially for poor countries. One of the chief problems of most modern African nations is finding funds to construct transportation links between their capitals and the rural areas and between inland agricultural and mineral areas and seaports.

C. Africa has relatively few internal barriers to communication

1. Compensating partly for the great distances is the fact that much of Africa consists of flat or rolling plains.
   Comparison. The American Midwest between the Alleghenies and the Rockies.

2. The Sahara Desert is the greatest obstacle to transcontinental communication; it is roughly as large as the entire United States. Yet it is an obstacle rather than a barrier; because of water holes and oases, caravan routes have traversed the desert from the time of Christ or before. On these routes camels still carry loads of salt, gold, ivory, spices, gum arabic, metal tools, glassware, and so forth. Much of West Africa's history can only be understood in the light of this vital trans-Saharan trade, upon whose profits

and taxation many African kings built great states and empires.

3. A second obstacle is that topographically Africa is composed of plateaus that drop rapidly near the the coasts to the sea. Rivers tumble down to the sea from the interior plateaus in rapids and waterfalls, so that few can be navigated from the coast inland. In many areas modern roads and railways must ascend sharply from the coast, increasing both the cost and the engineering problems of building them.

    Illustration. The continent is somewhat like a saucer turned upside down, higher on the east than the west.

4. There are several local obstacles to communication:

    a) The Atlas Mountain Chain (1,500 miles long) of Northwestern Africa. In history the Atlas has sheltered its indigenous Berber peoples from invasion and domination from the Mediterranean coast.

        Illustration. Show students a map of Africa, noting that in Morocco, Algeria, and Tunisia all major cities are located on the Atlantic or Mediterranean coast or on the coastal plain; there are no important cities in the Atlas mountains nor railways crossing them.

    b) Congo Rain Forest. Africa's largest area of swamps and dense vegetation; difficult to traverse except by the numerous rivers, which are tributaries to the great Congo River (second largest drainage area in the world).

        Illustration. Cite the film *The African Queen* as a fictional case in point. Demonstrate on the map that all the important cities of Zaire (formerly the Congo) are located on rivers, except for Lubumbushi, which is in drier country on the rich copper belt of the province of Katanga.

c) The Nile River's Sudd. A great swampy region in the modern Republic of Sudan where the Nile splits into hundreds of channels, choked with floating mats of papyrus-type reeds and grasses.

Illustration. Note on the map that there are no large cities in the southern part of the Sudan. Note also that this is the region in which the bloody civil war between the Moslem northern Sudanese and the non-Moslem southern Sudanese smoldered inconclusively for over fifteen years until 1972; the more powerful forces of the northern-dominated government could not be brought to bear effectively against the guerilla fighters of the south, because of the difficult terrain.

d) The Ethiopian Highlands. With elevations up to 15,000 feet, nearly half of Ethiopia is a rugged, inaccessible, yet reasonably fertile country, with a large population (more than 25,000,000). The ruggedness of the land has helped to protect the Ethiopian Christian civilization (founded in 350 A.D.) from surrounding Moslem neighbors and foreign invaders.

5. Despite these obstacles, the character of the topography has made it possible for peoples to move over vast areas and to remain in contact with each other. This has promoted a measure of unity in language

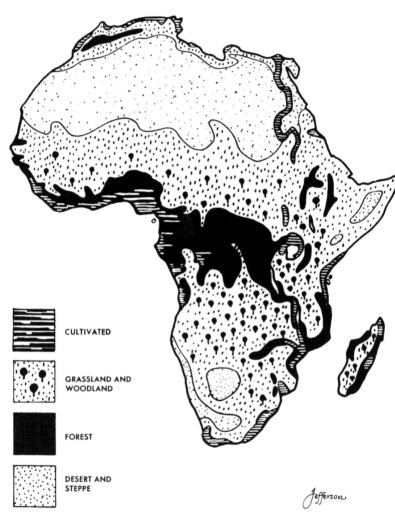

CULTIVATED

GRASSLAND AND
WOODLAND

FOREST

DESERT AND
STEPPE

Jefferson

Africa's vegetation and environmental zones

and culture, tempering the vast distances, so that there are evidences of deep roots of commonality among most African peoples.

Illustration. The Bantu-speaking peoples of central, eastern, and southern Africa, spread over an area of 5,000,000 sq. miles, with three to four hundred separate languages, still remain identifiably akin. Their languages are often more alike than Spanish and Portuguese; a Zulu can generally learn Luganda, spoken more than 2,000 miles away, within weeks.

D. Africa's climate is critically important

1. Temperatures, though warm, have little effect on the African people and their energy levels. The temperature in most of tropical Africa is relatively pleasant; cooling breezes in the evenings, cooler rainy seasons, and high evaporation rates bring relief.

   Comparisons. Compare the average July temperatures of important tropical African cities with major American cities.

   Compare a population density map (e.g. the Philips series recommended in the materials section) with the map of climate-vegetation zones; note that the warm areas near the equator are generally densely populated, implying a higher level of food production.

2. Temperatures do affect the soil fertility. Constant warmth accelerates the composition of vegetable matter in topsoil, retarding the buildup of humus, which is essential for rich and deep topsoil. The warm climate of tropical Africa aids the breed-

ing of disease-bearing insects and bacteria: the tsetse fly, which carries sleeping sickness (trypannosomiasis); the snail-borne bilharzia (schistosomiasis); the anopheles mosquito, which carries malaria; other mosquitoes that carry filariasis; the guinea worm, which causes blindness.

3.   Rainfall is the most critical climatic factor of all. More than half of Africa has too little annual rainfall to support good agriculture. Much of the remainder has barely enough rainfall, or the rain falls in heavy downpours during one season, leaving the land dry for the rest of the year. The heavy downpours help to *erode* the thin topsoils, carrying away the fertile part, while it also facilitates *leaching*, a process by which nutrients in the topsoil are washed downward through the soil, leaving the topsoil with inadequate nutrients.

Comparison. Compare the population density map with the climate-vegetation map, noting that the denser populations are in the areas of heavier rainfall.

Discussion. The several major vegetational and environmental zones (desert, rain forest, savanna grassland, dry forest-grassland, highland plateau, and Mediterranean zone) coincide with the incidence of rainfall. Populations tend to be denser in the rain forests of West Africa, the moister savannas, and the moist highlands of interior eastern Africa; the savanna is the largest region of important population concentration.

Because of thin topsoils and the slowness of soil to recover fertility after being cultivated for a few seasons, African farmers have worked out the *shifting plot* or *slash and burn* method of cultivation. Through this method, the farmer fells or rings the trees on a plot of several acres, allows them to dry, then burns them, together with all grass and underbrush; the ash is later mixed with the soil by hoe, adding chemical elements to it. Such a plot is sown for only a few seasons. When its fertility is depleted, the farmer moves on to an adjacent plot, then to another. After several years (often fifteen to twenty) he returns to the original plot, and the cycle begins again. This method, though seemingly wasteful of both land and natural vegetation, is remarkably well designed for the poor fertility conditions of most African soils; to improve on it would require long research and costly fertilizers, cover crops, and water storage facilities.

E. Africa has important mineral and energy resources
   1. Since ancient times Africans have profitably used their resources of iron, copper, gold, and tin.
       Illustration. Show students maps of ancient trade routes, exploited mineral deposits, and African kingdoms. (Books and maps recommended in history materials list show these routes and locations.)
   2. Modern African production of many minerals is responsible for a large percentage of the world's supply of gold, copper, iron, tin, manganese, uranium, cobalt, diamonds, bauxite, and other metals.
       Illustration. Discuss with students the tables (e.g., those in recommended geography texts such as that by William Hance) showing the African share of world production of minerals.

3. Energy sources are becoming increasingly important. Although coal, elsewhere a common source of energy, is not plentiful in Africa, oil is. Libya, Algeria, and Nigeria are among the world's major petroleum producers, and new deposits are being located and tapped in Angola, Mozambique, and other areas. Hydroelectric power from Africa's rapidly flowing rivers is a major actual and potential source of energy; Africa contains roughly forty percent of the world's hydroelectric potential. Many countries have already constructed huge dams and power stations, and more are projected to supply power for extracting metals from ores, operating textile and other factories, and a variety of consumer demands. Solar energy, while uneconomic for most uses, is thought to be a possible important power source for Africa in the future. When technology finds ways to harness the sun's power economically for such purposes as desalinizing sea water, parts of the Sahara might become cultivable. Africa's tropical location gives it a great advantage in solar rays.

F. Africa's diverse environments mean diversity of wealth and development

1. Even though we speak of and study "Africa," it is a huge continent of greatly varying environments.
   Illustration. Refer to the map of climate-vegetation zones and discuss with students the variations in rainfall, temperature, vegetation, crops, and way of life.

2. Africa has great variations among its population densities, distribution of mineral resources, areas of

fertile soil, energy supplies, and access to world transportation systems. Thus some nations are much more prosperous than others.

Illustration. Show students a table of per capita incomes of several richer and poorer African nations. Richer countries, such as Ghana, Nigeria, Zambia, and South Africa, benefit from their favorable soils, mineral deposits, timber growths, and energy sources. Poorer countries, such as Chad, Niger, and the Central African Republic, have large areas of aridity and low fertility and few known minerals.

3. The ways in which Africans have used their environments have varied historically. The countries just south of the Sahara were once the richest areas, when wealth came chiefly from trade across the Sahara. Today they are among the poorest in Africa because trade flows across the oceans, and they have fewer mineral resources. South Africa, today the wealthiest country in Africa, was once the poorest; today its vast mineral deposits and temperate climate have attracted millions of colonists from Europe and India who have grown prosperous because of the mineral riches of South Africa.

4. The deeply rooted, evolving relationship between the African and his land is an important, complex, easily underestimated phenomenon. For thousands of years Africans have been in the process of movement and change, even though that change has been relatively slower than comparable change in Europe. African methods of cultivation, the crops that are grown, and the patterns of settlement and ownership of land have been worked out over the centu-

ries by Africans; they do not readily accept change unless it seems consistent with their long experience and traditions. Africans have developed irrigation, methods of fertilization, and other agricultural techniques, and have changed these as conditions have required, in a long pattern of dynamic relationship with their environment. In some areas Africans have achieved enormously effective results; in others they have depleted previously poor soils and have created changes in their environment. Today, in an era of rapid, almost revolutionary change, the outside world must recognize the reality of the African attachment to the African environment and accept the fact that change must be controlled by the African, acting in the light of his unique experience. *Illustration.* Show the film *Two Life Styles in East Africa* (see materials list) to illustrate the effective control of the land of northern Tanzania by that area's farmers. Compare problems of erosion and over-grazing in parts of Africa, such as Senegal and South Africa, with the problems of Appalachia and the Oklahoma "dust bowl" area in the United States. Note the frequent conflict in Hollywood westerns between sheep herders and cattlemen, where the latter fear the former will deplete the soils because sheep graze the grass too closely.

G. Africa's topography and environmental zones
    Note: The following information need not be covered separately from the above; it is appended for the sake of completeness, since the student should emerge from his study of African geography with some sense of the most important features of the land and the major re-

gional environmental zones of Africa. This material is referred to, at least in part, in the above conceptual outline and can be utilized by the teacher along with the following points.

1. Mountains and Highlands

    a)   Atlas Mountains: serve to protect Berbers from unwanted outside influence; cause moisture-bearing air to precipitate on coastal plains, preventing Saharan-desert conditions from developing on coasts.

    b)   Highlands of Eastern Africa: stretch from northern Ethiopia to South Africa and Namibia; create cooler conditions and attract better rainfall.

    c)   Isolated mountains: several important volcanic mountains rise above the eastern highlands: Kilimanjaro, Kenya, Elgon, Meru. Each provides a unique environment with fertile soils from lava, good rainfall, cool climate on higher slopes.

       Illustration. More than 300,000 people (the Chagga) live on the slopes of Mt. Kilimanjaro and are among the most prosperous and progressive in Africa.

    d)   Drakensberg Mountains of South Africa and Lesotho: Africa's second largest range, after the Atlas; have afforded protection for Basuto people; provide considerable hydroelectric potential.

    e)   Small mountain ranges and massifs of western Africa: provide areas of cooler climate, better rainfall and soils, mineral resources; among the more important are the Ahaggar and Tibesti massifs of the Sahara, Futa Jallon and Guinea Highlands, Nimba Mountains of Guinea–Sierra Leone–Liberia, Jos Plateau of Nigeria, Mount Cameroon and Cameroon Highlands.

2. Lakes: Generally important for fishing, transport, and source of water.

    a) East African Great Lakes: one group, formed by the Western Rift system (see below, 5), is long, narrow, deep, useful for fishing and transport and includes Lakes Edward, Albert, Kivu, Tanganyika, and Malawi. Another group, formed by the Great Rift system (see below, 5), is shallow and alkaline. Some that are poor for fishing or water supply but yield minerals include Lakes Rudolph, Naivasha, Natron, Manyara, Eyasi, and Rukwa.

    b) Lake Chad, central Africa

    c) Lake Tana, Ethiopia, source of Blue Nile

    d) Lake Nyanza (Victoria), East Africa, world's second largest, in a basin between the two rifts; high evaporation rate helps insure good rains for surrounding lands.

    e) Numerous swampy, shallow lakes of southern Zaire, Zambia, Botswana, and Angola.

3. Rivers: Useful as water sources, irrigation, fishing, transport.

    a) Nile: 4,160 miles long

    b) Congo: 2,900 miles

    c) Niger: 2,600 miles

    d) Zambezi: 1,600 miles

    e) Senegal: 1,000 miles

    f) Volta: 700 miles

g) Gambia: 500 miles
4. Deserts
   a) Sahara: world's largest, approximately 3,000,000 sq. miles. Much of the Sahara is incapable of supporting life, but many parts have springs, underground water near the surface, or barely enough rainfall to support grasses or other vegetation. Oases are intensively farmed, while drier areas provide hardy grasses where pastoral nomads herd camels, sheep, and goats.
   b) Kalahari, together with the Namib: southern Africa, some areas of complete barrenness, others where a few inches of rain fall once a year, causing grasses to grow briefly. During this season wild game enters to graze, followed by Bushmen hunters.
5. The Rift Systems
   a) A massive folding of the earth's surface caused a long rift, the Great Rift, averaging more than 30 miles in width and with depths up to 3,000 feet, running from the Sea of Galilee through the Red Sea, Ethiopia, eastern Africa, and out into the Indian Ocean between Mozambique and Madagascar. This rift is generally less fertile and more arid than the plateau through which it cuts.
   b) West of the Great Rift runs a shorter but deeper rift, from Ethiopia down to Lake Malawi where it rejoins the Great Rift. In the Western Rift are the deep, narrow Great Lakes, some a depth of more than 5,000 feet below the adjacent plateau. Lake Tanganyika is the second deepest lake in the world (after Baikal in

the U.S.S.R.). Cutting through volcanic country, the Western Rift is bordered by some very fertile, densely populated lands, such as western Uganda, Burundi, and Rwanda.

6. Major Environmental Zones

   a) Mediterranean: extreme northwestern and southern tips of Africa; cool, moist winters; warm, dry summers; moderately fertile soils; major crops: wheat, grapes, olives, peaches, apples, citrus fruits, cork, truck vegetables, barley.

   b) Desert: see above, 4.

   c) Savannas: moderate rainfall (20–50 inches per year), few large trees, typically grasses of various types plus acacia trees and hardy shrubs. A major savanna area borders the southern edge of the Sahara, all across Africa, extending south into Sudan, Central African Republic, Cameroun. Other large savannas cover parts of eastern Zaire, Zambia, East Africa, Botswana, South Africa, and Rhodesia.

   d) Savanna–dry forests: frequently overlapping with savannas, especially in central, eastern, and southern Africa; roughly similar rain and vegetation patterns, except for stands of hardwood trees, not densely spaced, which often shed leaves during the dry season. Both the savanna and savanna–dry forest have mildly fertile soils, with occasional richer areas (e.g., Kano area of northern Nigeria), and produce millet, sorghum, corn, some root crops (potatoes, cassava), cotton, shea nuts, citrus fruits, vegetables, wild honey, peanuts, beans, water-melons, rice and tobacco.

e) Rain forest: heavy rainfall (60 inches or more per year), very tall hardwood trees (e.g., mahogany, ebony), moderate to heavy underbrush. Two major regions: West Africa between savanna and Atlantic; Congo River basin. Moderately fertile soils, although leaching is a serious problem in places. Relatively densely populated, especially in West Africa. Major crops: root crops (yams, cassava, taro, manioc, guinea yam), some corn, tropical fruits, citrus fruits, bananas and plantains, leafy vegetables, cocoa, rubber.

f) Highlands: the entire highland area of eastern Africa, from Ethiopia to South Africa; resembles the savanna and savanna–dry woodland zones, but altitude means cooler climates and slightly higher rainfall. Soils occasionally volcanic and fertile. Major crops: wheat, millet, corn, cotton, coffee, tea, bananas, truck vegetables, potatoes, tobacco. The highlands have attracted European settlers more than any other region except parts of the Mediterranean because of their cooler climate.

Teaching Materials

The following suggestions and recommendations should be considered only after the teacher has read the Introduction and Chapter Nine, which cover teaching strategies, curriculum design, and criteria for the evaluation of materials.

Budget resources will naturally be a critical criterion in deciding which of the specific materials to purchase. Africa is but one of a number of vital regional cultural areas in a school's intercultural education program. Although a number of free and inexpensive materials are listed, they are not generally produced specifically for classroom use. However, they can be used as supplements to basic maps, texts, reference books, and audio-visual materials.

The following materials and sources would provide a very comprehensive collection if a school were fortunate enough to be able to purchase or rent everything listed. Since that is impossible in most cases, asterisks indicate basic materials without which it would be almost impossible to present a unit on African geography. The teacher is urged, however, to go as far beyond these minimal recommendations as budgets permit.

African geography is normally the first aspect of African life American students learn about in their schools. It may be taught by elementary education specialists or by subject area specialists. First impressions last the longest. Careful selection of materials for African geography is critical.

BASIC TEXTS AND REFERENCES
(For libraries and teacher reference)

Africa, A New Geographic Survey by E. Mountjoy and M. Embleton. Surveys entire continent, general introduction. Praeger Publishers, 111 Fourth Ave., New York, N.Y. 10003. 1969. $10.

Africa South of the Sahara by A. T. Grove. A good general geography with physical, cultural, and economic geography covered. Limited by its exclusion of Northern Africa. Oxford University Press, 200 Madison Ave., New York, N.Y. 10016. 1968. $9.

Africa: The Geography of a Changing Continent by J. M. Pritchard. Mr. Pritchard is a British geographer writing for the English-speaking African market. The book is directed to upper senior high or survey level courses in college. Thematically organized, it can be useful to upper elementary and junior high school teachers introducing African geography. Africana Publishing Corporation, 101 Fifth Ave., New York, N.Y. 10003. $6.50.

Focus on Geography edited by Phillip Bacon. Series of essays designed to introduce major concepts and teaching strategies in geography education. National Council for Geographic Education, 1201 Sixteenth St., N.W., Washington, D.C. 20036. 1970. $5.50. pap.

The Geography of Modern Africa by William Hance. A good general text, emphasizing contemporary economic geography and modern economic, industrial, and agricultural development and resources. Data is dated but remains a useful survey. Columbia University Press, 562 West 113th St., New York, N.Y. 10025. 1964. $15.

INEXPENSIVE SUPPLEMENTAL MATERIALS

Tourist and African Government Information

Most African governments cannot afford to produce large quantities of free materials for distribution in America. What is available can be very helpful, if used judiciously and creatively, even though the variety is limited and the materials were generally not produced with schools in mind. The following African missions in the United States will send teachers some free publications and materials.

The materials will show only certain aspects of a country. Naturally, they are the ones Africans are most proud of and seek to develop. This does not negate their value or truth. It simply means you have to try to find other things to produce a broader view of African realities.

☐ Embassy of Ghana, Information Section, 2460 Sixteenth St., N.W., Washington, D.C. 20009

☐ Kenya Tourist Board, 15 East 51st. St., New York, N.Y. 10017

☐ Morocco Tourist Board, 597 Fifth Ave., New York, N.Y. 10017

☐ Permanent Mission of Ghana to the United Nations, 144 East 44th St., New York, N.Y. 10017

☐ Permanent Mission of Nigeria to the United Nations, 757 Third Ave., New York, N.Y. 10017

☐ Permanent Mission of Zambia to the United Nations, 150 East 58th St., New York, N.Y. 10022

☐ U.A.R. Tourist Board, 630 Fifth Ave., New York, N.Y. 10022

☐ Zambia Tourist Board, 970 Third Ave., New York, N.Y. 10017

Picture Sets

Scenes of children and family life in Africa are available for elementary level educators. These materials are produced to illustrate the work of international assistance organizations. Inexpensive sets may also contain scenes from Asia or Latin America, which may be used for comparative and contrasting purposes.

The pictures were not produced with teachers specifically in mind. Your task is to adapt them to classroom objectives.

For students who seem to have trouble reading texts they can be valuable. Sharpen students' skills of visual inquiry and reasoning if their reading level does not correspond to the materials provided by the school system.

United Nations Association of the U.S.A., 345 East 46th St., New York, N.Y. 10017. Emphasis on children and family life. Color and black and white. $1 to $2 per set.

United Nations Sales Office, United Nations, First Ave. and 42nd St., New York, N.Y. 10017. African, Asian, and Latin American themes. Color and black and white. $1 to $2 per set.

United States Committee to UNICEF, 331 East 38th St., New York, N.Y. 10017. Children and family life. Color and black and white. $1.

Educators seeking information and curriculum assistance for the K-8 level should contact the Children's Information Center of this organization. It produces listings of materials for library purchase and has recently developed several unique short units for the study of other cultures. The Center is the best source of information in the United States on children from Asia, Africa, and Latin America.

General and Economic Data

Monthly Economic Review. Economic and trade data. Use school letterhead when requesting, but even so it may be difficult to obtain since the reviews are produced for a commercial clientele. Barclays Bank, D.C. & O., 49th St. and Park Ave., New York, N.Y. 10017. Free.

Monthly Economic Review. Same type data and cautions as above. Standard Bank, 2 Wall St., New York, N.Y. 10001. Free.

State Department Notes. Four- to six-page summaries for

each country in Africa. Order by names of countries.
High school and adult reading level. Government Printing Office, Washington, D.C. 20402. $.10 per summary.
World Population Analysis. Detailed statistical reviews on
health, economy, population, and the like. Suitable for
high school use. Population Reference Bureau, 1755
Massachusetts Ave., N.W., Washington, D.C. 20036.
$.50.

Stamps, Coins, and Postcards

These items are especially useful for grades 4–9. A good
set of African stamps or coins can be assembled for $5 and
less and are effective teaching aids for younger and middle
school children. Most local stamp and coin dealers will as-
semble sets for you, and you can choose the most interesting
from his collections and catalogs. If you prefer, write:
Stamps and Coins International, 829 Second Ave., New
York, N.Y. 10017.

There is a kit containing thirty-five East African postcards,
which show different scenes and activities in Kenya, Uganda,
and Tanzania to be used with a map exercise keyed to the
cards, large pictures of East African presidents, and a bibliography of readings for teachers interested in the area. The
cards should give teachers a good trigger device to get students to react to visual phenomena as they start an African
unit. African-American Institute, 866 United Nations Plaza,
New York, N.Y. 10017. $4.95 per set, prepaid.

Postcards and stamps give students things to touch and
exchange. They are a piece of Africa. They can be adapted
to traditional styles of classroom instruction in which all
students do the same thing, or in an open classroom they

can be assigned to individual students with particular assignments.

A useful listing of free and inexpensive materials on Africa can be found in the pamphlet *Studying Africa* by L. Kentworthy, Teachers College Press, 1234 Amsterdam Ave., New York, 10027. $1.95.

MORE EXPENSIVE AIDS

Maps

Africa Inquiry Maps. An unusual and very sound new product developed by Project Africa, a U.S. Office of Education financed curriculum project at Carnegie-Mellon University. Using an inquiry approach, the transparencies and teacher guides enable students to work at their own pace. Sunburst Communications, Pound Ridge, N.Y. 10576. $43.

Heritage of Africa. An ethnolinguistic map, paper. The National Geographic Society, 17th and M Sts., N.W., Washington, D.C. 20036. $2.

°Imperial Map of Africa (28″ x 42″). Color, paper. Rand McNally. $1.

°Philips Africa Series. An excellent set of five cloth maps mounted on a durable tripod. Set covers physical geography and landforms, climates, vegetation, population density, and political geography. Produced by the Philips firm in Britain for the African school market. Denoyer-Geppert, $60.

°Regional Economic Atlas of Africa. Color, paper. Oxford University Press, 200 Madison Ave., New York, N.Y. 10016. $7.50.

Major Map Producers

Denoyer-Geppert Company, Box 93550, Chicago, Ill. 60690
Hammond Map Company, Division of McGraw-Hill, 1121
    Sixth Ave., New York, N.Y. 10036
A. J. Nystrom Company, 3333 Elston Ave., Chicago, Ill.
    60618
Rand McNally & Company, Box 7600, Chicago, Ill. 60680

Major Transparency Producers

Aevec Company, 500 Fifth Ave., New York, N.Y. 10036
Allyn-Bacon Company, 470 Atlantic Ave., Boston, Mass.
    02210
Keuffel and Esser Company, 300 Adams St., Hoboken, N.J.
    07030
McGraw-Hill Company, 1121 Sixth Ave., New York, N.Y.
    10036

Filmstrips

Note to Teacher: Please review criteria for selection and
evaluation of films in Chapter Nine before ordering films or
filmstrips for review, purchase, or rental. In the Appendix is
a list of twenty-six producers of filmstrips on Africa. Most
of these companies have products that cover some aspects
of African geography.

Africa, Focus on East Africa. 1970. Grades 4–9. Three film-
    strips with records, color: "A Farmer in Tanzania," "A
    Fishing Village in Tanzania," and "An African Com-
    munity: The Masai." Bailey Film Associates. Each strip,
    $8; each record, $5; boxed $39; with cassettes, each $7;
    boxed $45.

This series concentrates on relationships between men and
their environment. The narration is concise and nicely

paced. Human beings are introduced, and their life-styles are explored with reference to their immediate surroundings. The strip on the Masai, while reinforcing certain stereotypes of this much maligned and examined group of human beings, is sensibly done. Yet the breadth and variety of Masai life will have to be developed with other sources.

Africa Focus on Economy. 1970. Grades 4–8. Five filmstrips with records, 40 frames each, color: "African Markets," "Transportation in Africa," "Foods of Tropical Africa," "Industry in Africa," and "City Life in Africa." Bailey Film Associates. Each strip $8; each record $5; boxed $65; with cassettes, each $7; boxed $60.

These strips are carefully narrated with little information overload. They focus on West Africa but are relevant for other sections of the continent. Their themes are carefully and logically developed. Children have time to react. Strips have no captions, and the narration is right to the point.

Africa Regional Geography Series. 1967. Grades 7–9. Six filmstrips, no record, B&W: "The Continent of Africa," "The Economy of Africa," "Northern Africa," "West Africa," "East Africa," and "Southern Africa." McGraw-Hill Company. $40 per set.

If you are looking for a traditional set of media based on a regional approach, this product can be considered. The captions may disappoint some teachers. The filmstrip on Southern Africa runs for eighteen frames before one views an African. Yet when compared to the filmstrips of its competitors, Encyclopaedia Britannica and Society for Visual Education, which have also produced a group of regional studies, this set may meet more of your needs.

Africa's Children. 1972. Middle grades. Six filmstrips with records or cassettes, color: "Life in an African Fishing Village," "Life in an African Seacoast City," "Life in an East African City," "Life in an African Farming Village," "Life near an African Game Reserve," and "Life in an African Tribal Village." Scott Education. Set with records, $69; with cassettes, $75.

This series is good for peer group studies as it shows children and family life in six geographically and culturally distinct areas of the continent. Only the final filmstrip seems inappropriately designed. The use of the term "tribal" is not explained, and it is not clear why this word was not used with the other African life-styles, which are also agriculturally oriented. However, the series, on the whole, is worthy of preview. Includes a teacher's guide.

West Africa Today. 1973. Grades 7–12. Four filmstrips with records or cassettes, color: "An Introduction to West Africa," "Village Life in West Africa," "City Life in West Africa," and "Arts and Crafts of West Africa." Contemporary Media Inc. Sets with records or cassettes, $69.50; individual strips with record or cassette, $19.50.

A diverse approach to contemporary West Africa that is recommended for purchase preview. This product was produced by Professor Barry Beyer, Director of Project Africa, a secondary curriculum development project located at Carnegie-Mellon University. The materials were developed by Dr. Beyer and his colleagues during a recent study tour in West Africa.

Films

From 1967 through 1970 the educational film market on Africa was inundated. Picking your way through the mass of films is treacherous. Relics from the mid-1930s remain on the market. Exciting new films come out from small companies lacking national marketing organizations, and hence you may not hear about them. Be very careful and try to see as many offerings as possible at professional gatherings or on preview. Addresses of producers and rental libraries are given in the Appendix.

The Continent of Africa. 15 min., color, 1966. McGraw-Hill Company. $205; rental, $15. This does bifurcate the continent into misconceptions called tropical Africa or sub-Saharan Africa. A good introductory film that carefully balances elements of change with those of traditional life.

INDUSTRIAL AND URBAN FOCUS

African City, Contrasting Cultures. 11 min., color, 1970. Bailey Film Associates. $145. A superb film showing colonial impact and the African response. The teacher should look up basic facts on the Ivory Coast before using it. Otherwise, he will never be able to explain the official city band of Lyons, France, parading down the main street in Abidjan. Social class stratification and economic specialization are emphasized but in a soft way. The film does not hit hard. The teacher can take it any way his ideological persuasion goes.

Economic Development in an African Country. 11½ min., color, 1968. Bailey Film Associates. $145. A promotional film originally done by United Africa Ltd., a British-owned company with extensive industrial and agricultural investment in West Africa. If this turns you off, then look elsewhere, but if you are eclectic, look at this film. It shows the relationships between rural and urban Nigeria. The focus is on manufacturing and the development of service industries. Naturally, the film is optimistic and unmindful of industrial effects on Nigerian life.

Industry in Africa. 11½ min., color, 1970. Bailey Film Associates. $150. Scenes of industrial growth, urbanization, and African working-class life are featured. Useful to show non-White-collar urban African life.

THEMATIC FILMS

Mali and the Desert. 15 min., B&W, 1964. Crowell, Collier-Macmillan. $85, sale; $6, rental from Association Films. An Alastair Cooke-narrated effort produced for the UN. Strong emphasis on interaction between men and their environment. Narration is careful and accurate. Although nine years old, the film's message is timeless.

Rainy Season in West Africa. 14 min., color, 1966. Films Incorporated. $190 (sale only). A tightly edited view of agricultural life in the grasslands of West Africa. The focus is on village life and the rhythms of human existence related to the wet and dry seasons.

Water and Man in North Africa. 16 min., color, 1966. McGraw-Hill Company. $210, sale; $15, rental. The market is flooded with the "oasis-date" type of film. This is one recommended for preview.

Water on the Savanna. 20 min., color, 1970. Texture Films. $240, sale; $20, rental from Texture Films. Shot in Niger, this film skillfully covers many of the same themes as *Mali and the Desert,* but it is more narrowly focused on village life and efforts to stabilize the supply and security of water. The work of a Nigerien film-maker.

School systems that want to actively involve their K-6 students in learning about an African culture by using realia and artifacts from that culture should investigate the *Ashanti Family of Ghana Kit*. It contains a teacher resource guide, 15 children's books produced in Ghana (in English), 20 study prints (11″ x 14″), materials for duplication and handout, two filmstrips depicting Ashanti life in Ghana, a pre-recorded audio cassette containing songs and Ashanti legends, three magnetic compasses, cocoa beans, and six artifacts. These materials and their use are based on the Family of Man Social Studies Project for the Elementary Grades developed at the University of Minnesota in 1972. The *Kit* is available from Selective Educational Equipment Inc., 3 Bridge St., Newton, Mass. 02195 for $174. This is a major school purchase that can be used in classrooms throughout a school. It comes in a carrying-storage case.

The following films should be considered for preview. They concern African family activity and African youth— themes that emerge in studies of social geography.

Many American film companies distribute titles showing African urban families. Most of these focus on very atypical families. Parents tend to be highly educated and very affluent. They do not reflect the typical family life of urban Africans. Films of this type are made because they portray life-styles recognizable by some American children. These comments do not negate the value and potential utility of these films.

African Odyssey: The Two Worlds of Musembe. 15 min., color, 1971. Learning Corporation of America. $195, sale; $15, rental. Musembe is a Kenyan African, about eleven years old, who lives in Nairobi. His father is a government civil servant who has to make a journey to his home in western Kenya. Description of urban and rural life-styles is well done. Children watching the film might be asked to play the role of a youth in the farming village to which Musembe and his father return. What do they think of Musembe?

Family of the City, Growing up in Nairobi. 11 min., color, 1971. McGraw-Hill Company. $160, sale; $16, rental. Two young boys, seven and ten years old, live in the city. Their father is a radio announcer. Film describes their home and activities and has many excellent shots of the social diversity of Nairobi, the capital of Kenya. Film is narrated by the older boy.

Growing up in Tunis. 14 min., color, 1970. Universal Films. $180 (sale only). The only North African film of its type. Depicts a boy of about eleven growing up in the cosmopolitan city of Tunis on the Mediterranean. His father is an import-export merchant. The family has a city apartment and a house in a coastal village. Comparisons can be made of this child's life-style and future opportunities and those of the Berber Tunisian youth and society shown in the last third of film.

While films of African urban life tend to identify families and children personally with names, those describing rural life rarely do so. Rural Africans are regarded as "outsiders." Rural Africans do not speak to us except through a narrator. Teachers should point this out and caution children about viewing African society through a microscope as one would study fauna or flora. The fault is ours. We are unable to speak African languages and hence use an English narrator or operate on an inquiry basis.

"African Village Life," series of eleven color films, 1969. International Film Foundation. This is a sound *but no narration* series. It is totally inquiry oriented. The producer states "I believe that children like to be left alone to make their own discoveries." The films achieve their purpose. *Building a Boat* (Bozo), 7 min., $90; *Herding Cattle* (Peul), 7 min., $90; *Onion Farming* (Dogon), 7 min., $90; *Building a House* (Bozo), 7 min., $90; *Hunting Wild Doves* (Dogon), 7 min., $90; *Cotton Growing and Spinning* (Dogon), 7 min., $90; *Daily Life of the Bozo*, 15 min., $150; *Fishing on the Niger River* (Bozo), 17 min., $175; *Magic Rites: Divination by Chicken Sacrifice* (Dogon), 7 min., $90; *Annual Festival of the Dead* (Dogon), 14 min., $150. All focus on African societies in the West African state of Mali. It is recommended that teachers carefully preview these films before use. All are worth previewing. You can then choose the theme best related to your needs.

River People of Chad. 20 min., color, 1966. Films Incorporated. $260 (sale only). Family unity and survival in the grasslands of West Africa are emphasized. The Africans are not personalized. Students can be asked to project their thoughts and self-identity. Scenes of Fort Lamy, capital of Chad, can be used for comparative and contrasting exercises with the agricultural-riverine culture.

Two Life Styles in East Africa. 18½ min., color, 1970. Bailey Film Associates. $240. Two families in Tanzania are shown in a typical day. One lives in a coastal, fishing village on the Indian Ocean. The other farms in the highlands some four hundred miles inland. Film effectively relates working patterns, life-styles, and economic development to climate, topography, and the influence of the monetary economy. The narration can be turned off. The film "works" using a total inquiry system.

Study Print Sets

Africa. Sixteen color pictures on medium weight paper, 18″ × 30″. Denoyer-Geppert Company, 5235 Ravenswood Ave., Chicago, Ill. 60640. $43, with frame; $30, without frame.

African Cities. Twenty-four page, black and white pictures in heavy binder with spiral backing. John Day Company, 287 Park Ave. South, New York, N.Y. 10019. $21.

Living in Kenya. Twelve color pictures in durable, heavy material, 19″ × 23″, with a teacher's manual. Silver Burdette, Box 362, Morristown, N.J. 07960. $14.95.

PROFESSIONAL RESOURCES

For continuing information about geographic education methods and materials consult these:

Focus. Grades 7–12. Occasional issues on Africa. Surveys individual countries. Adult reading level. American Geographical Society, Broadway and 156th St., New York, N.Y. 10027. Monthly, $.50 each.

Journal of Geography. National Council for Geographic Education, Room 1226, 111 West Washington St., Chicago, Ill. 60602. 9 issues, $12.

Social Education. National Council for the Social Studies, 1201 Sixteenth St., N.W., Washington, D.C. 20036. 9 issues, $10.

2 African history I: from human origins to the period of European influence

It is traditional, in most survey approaches to African history, to begin with the origin and evolution of man. Although this topic is far removed from the more familiar study of known societies, states, and events, it can be included in the study of African history. Anthropology does tend to interest many students.

Today it is also traditional to devote some attention to developments in Africa that pre-date European contact or that were little influenced by the European contact after the fifteenth century. For many years African history was seen largely as the history of European contact with Africa, it being assumed that most of Africa either had no prior history or that its history might never be reconstructed. The more modern approach, which this handbook follows, is to help students understand that Africa has had a long and varied history, within which the great changes that followed European contact and conquest were but a recent chain of events.

The present chapter treats African history up to the period 1450–1850, largely omitting European influence, which was unimportant in most of Africa before the past few centuries. Chapter Three treats the period from about 1450–1850 (the date varies with the area of Africa being considered) up to the present—a time in which European influence has been involved in major changes in Africa.

Neither chapter attempts to summarize the myriad events, developments, and achievements of thousands of years of African history. Each chapter begins with an outline that combines chronology with geographic area and summarizes the topics that are often covered in traditional surveys of African history. These outlines are intended for teacher reference only; many teachers prefer not to follow a chronological sequence, and most will find that they do not have sufficient time to cover the entire outline in any case.

Following the outline in each chapter is a summary discussion of the major forces, themes, and problems that characterized African development during the period covered by the outline. If a chronological approach for all of Africa is followed, this summary will provide the teacher with a summation of the factors that influenced development. If a chronological approach is not used, many teachers will find it effective to examine African history through the framework of these summaries of forces (e.g., the influence of Islam on African political systems, economies, or trade). And, if a teacher selects one area or period for special attention, the chronological outline will help to put it into a broad perspective, while the summary will provide a framework for study.

OUTLINE:
Prehistory to 1450–1850

A. Human Origins and Evolution
    Africa is the probable homeland of man's earliest an-

cestors, from the origins of the great apes on through
the now familiar sequence of Australopithecus, Pithe-
canthropus, Neanderthal, to modern man. Anthropological finds in South Africa, Tanzania, Kenya, and Ethiopia
provide a panorama of human evolution.

B. African Prehistory: The Stone Ages
Since 2,000,000 B.C. tools made by man and his proto-
human ancestors reveal an evolution of technology
in Africa. This evolution was not uniform over the
continent; most Africans had entered the Iron Age
long before the time of Christ, while a few practiced
Stone Age manufacture and ways of life up until the
past century.

C. The Peopling of Africa
1. Although there is too little information available to
trace the precise origins and migrations of human
races, Africa has long provided a home to Cauca-
soids, Negroids, Bushmanoids, and Pygmoids. Their
major areas of historic concentration can be identified, and some study of their movements and mix-
tures is possible.

2. For thousands of years peoples have migrated and
mixed with each other, so that there are few societies that are racially pure. Tracing some of the
main mixture-contacts, such as those across the
Sahara Desert, in the Ethiopian highlands, in the
Nile Valley, and in the path of the great Bantu migrations, provides a useful background to an understanding of early African history.

D. African Peoples and Cultures
The peoples of Africa are heterogeneous in race, language, economy, and social organization. Yet they do
fall into certain broad categories, which are useful to

provide an overview of the major concentrations of peoples. Once this overview is clear, a study of individual societies becomes more meaningful. There are several ways in which the peoples of Africa are frequently categorized or classified:

1. Language

    Although there are hundreds of identifiably separate languages spoken, they group into several large stocks. There is not, however, a complete correlation between language and way of life. One people speaking a Bantu language, for example, may practice semi-nomadic pastoralism, while another, speaking a closely related Bantu language, may be settled farmers. For this reason, other means of classifying are desirable.

    a) Afro-Asiatic includes most languages of northern Africa, the Nile Valley, and northeastern Africa as well as Arabic and Hebrew.

    b) Congo-Kordofanian includes most languages spoken in western Africa south of the Sahara as well as the Bantu languages of central and southern Africa.

    c) Sudanic includes the languages of the upper Nile, the adjacent Sahara and sudanic grasslands, and part of the heart of central Africa.

    d) Several smaller stocks that may be distantly related to Sudanic or Congo-Kordofanian (Songhaic, Maban, Furian).

    e) Khoisan includes the languages of the Bushmen and Hottentots.

2. Economy

    The peoples of Africa are also grouped according to

Africa's major language families

their predominant economic activity, which coin-
cides roughly with the continent's environmental
zones. Thus peoples of the sudanic grasslands of
western and central Africa grow millet, sorghum,
and certain other basic crops, tending livestock as a
supplement. Peoples of the western rain forests and
the Congo basin depend upon the cultivation of
tuberous crops, such as yams, cassava, and taro,
with minor reliance on livestock. In central, eastern,
and southern Africa there are large zones where
primary reliance is on cattle herding, with the growing of millet. sorghum, and maize as a secondary or
minor activity.

Economic classification is helpful, but again does
not serve as an all-inclusive tool. Many peoples
practice mixed economies in the midst of areas of
pastoralism or grain farming, and economy varies
as the rainfall, soils, and other environmental conditions vary.

3. Socio-Political Organization
    Even less useful, yet not without classification value
    are arrangements of African peoples by their pre-
    dominant form of socio-political organization. Thus
    many live in highly organized states, headed by a
    divine or semi-divine king; some live in small family
    bands, with no system of government; others live in
    local clan groupings, with no centralized authority,
    still others live in tribal groupings, headed by a
    chief or council. Many other kinds of social organi-
    zation can be used to classify African peoples: ex-
    amples are clan structure, matrilineal or patrilineal
    descent, or age grading.

4. Geographic Distribution

The most consistent means of classification is simply by area. Generally the peoples of a given area speak the same or related languages, practice similar economies, and use similar forms of socio-political organization. Yet even a geographic classification is far from perfect. Within a large area there may be significant variations in environment that influence how the people live; there have been constant migrations in the course of African history; and many aspects of culture have diffused from one area to another. The following broad zones are useful for classifying cultural areas, however:

a) North Africa: the coastal and Atlas region
b) North Africa: the Sahara
c) Nile Valley
d) Ethiopian Highlands
e) Western Africa: the sudanic grasslands
f) Western Africa: the rain forests
g) Eastern Sudan (Lake Chad to Nile)
h) Horn of Africa (lowland Ethiopia, Somalia, parts of East Africa)
i) Bantu-speaking Africa: Central, Eastern, and Southern Africa
  i) Congo forests
  ii) Central savannas
  iii) Highlands of Zambia, Rhodesia, Mozambique
  iv) Southern Africa
  v) Indian Ocean coast
  vi) Great Lakes and East Africa

The recommended materials at the end of the history chapters employ this classification, in general. Several sketch out the distribution of languages, economies, socio-political organizations, and culture patterns that characterize these regions. In addition, the materials list contains recommended studies of individual societies within most of these regions, for use in those courses that take a generally anthropological approach to African study. For an overview, the teacher is urged to consult E. J. Murphy's *History of African Civilization* (see materials list).

E. Periods of African History: A Chronology

1. 15,000–5000 B.C.: Agricultural Origins

    Conventionally, African agriculture is said to have begun in Egypt about 5000 B.C. Recent research has shown, however, that the picture is less clear. Possibly the Africans of the Sahara practiced both grain collection and grain cultivation as early as 6000 B.C., and the peoples of the Upper Nile of Nubia (modern Republic of Sudan) apparently collected grain and ground it into flour or meal as early as 15,000–12,000 B.C. Probably later than the Egyptian adoption of agriculture, the peoples of several other areas began cultivation between about 4000 and 1000 B.C.

    a) Western Sudan (modern Mali-Mauritania-Senegal): between 4000 and 1000 B.C.
    b) North Africa: 3000–1500 B.C.
    c) Ethiopia: 2500–1000 B.C.

2. 5000 B.C.–200 A.D: The Nile

    Egyptian civilization originated in the Lower Nile and developed rapidly in the period 4500–1500 B.C. Its gradual decline was followed by the rule of

Libya, Nubia, Persia, Greece, and Rome. The Nubian civilization of Kush, which later became the Meroitic civilization, developed between 2000 and 500 B.C. Between 500 B.C. and 200 .A.D., it flourished around its capital of Meroe, in the modern Republic of Sudan.

3. 1000 B.C.–1000 A.D.: Outside the Nile Valley
    a) West Africa: the high cultures of Tichitt, Mauritania (1200 B.C.–300 B.C.) and Nok, Nigeria (900 B.C.–200 A.D.); foundations of Ghana, Tekrur, and Kanem-Bornu
    b) North Africa: the Phoenician settlement and the creation of Carthage (1000–150 B.C.); Greek Cyrenaica (Libya); Roman North Africa; the Vandal conquest (428–522 A.D.); the Byzantine Christian Empire; Arabization after the seventh century.
    c) The Christian states of Nubia (500–1500 A.D.)
    d) Ethiopia: The foundation of Axum 500 B.C.–200 A.D.); the growth of Christianity after the fourth century; the Empire, 300–1000 A.D.
    e) The Bantu: origins in Nigeria-Cameroun area; migrations to Katanga (200 B.C.–100 A.D.); expansion throughout subequatorial Africa (100–1000 A.D.)

4. 1000–1900 A.D.
    a) Muslim North Africa: the conquest of Spain and Portugal; the flowering of Tunisia, Algeria, and Morocco; Egypt as a Muslim center; the Almoravid and Almohad movements; the Turkish-Mamluk conquest and the North African decline.

Major states, empires, and power centers circa 1800 A.D.

b) The Sudanic states and empires: the origins, growth, and decline of numerous powerful kingdoms in the grasslands of the West African interior between 200 and 1900 A.D.

   i) Ancient Tekrur and Ghana (200–1100) in modern Senegal and Mauritania

   ii) The successor empires of Mali and Songhai (1200–1600) in modern Senegal, Mali, and Niger.

   iii) The long-lived empire of Kanem-Bornu around Lake Chad (100–1850).

   iv) The powerful Hausa city-states of northern Nigeria (1400–1900)

   v) The states of Bagirmi and Wadai in the far interior, east of Lake Chad (1500–1900)

   vi) The Mossi states of Upper Volta (1300–1900)

   vii) The Wolof states of Senegal (1400–1800)

   viii) Later states of the Mande-speaking peoples of Senegal and Mali (1600–1900)

   ix) The spread over western Africa of the Fulani peoples, their leadership in Islamic revival movements, and their empire in Nigeria (1800–1900)

   x) The Yoruba empire of Oyo (1500–1800)

c) The forest states of West Africa: the rise to power, after 1500, of new states and empires in the great West African rain forests.

   i) Denkyira and Akwamu (1500–1650)

   ii) The Asante empire of modern Ghana (1600–1900)

  iii) The Yoruba states of southern Nigeria (1600–1900)

  iv) The empire of Benin in southern Nigeria (1300–1900)

  v) The kingdom of Dahomey (1600–1900)

d) The origins and development of the Bantu-speaking peoples (500 B.C.–1900 A.D.)

  i) West African origins and migrations to central and southern Africa

  ii) The powerful states of Angola and Zaire: Kongo, Luba, Lunda, and Kuba (1300–1800)

  iii) States and empires of Rhodesia and Zambia: Mwene Mutapa, Zimbabwe, Lozi, and Bemba (1400–1900)

  iv) The states of Southern Africa: Zulu, Xhosa, and Basotho (1700–1880)

  v) The Swahili civilization of the Indian Ocean coast (1000–1900)

  vi) The interlacustrine states of East Africa: Buganda, Bunyoro, Burundi, and Rwanda (1350–1900)

e) The civilizations of the Horn of Northeast Africa.

  i) The origins and development of ancient Axum (500 B.C.–1000 A.D.), the development of a Christian civilization, and the development of the Ethiopian empire

  ii) Galla migrations and conflicts between Amhara and Galla in Ethiopia (1400–1800)

  iii) Expansion of the Somali and the growth of Islamic sultanates (1000–1800)

iv) The Nilotic migrations and conquests (1400–1700) from the Sudan into East Africa

This highly abbreviated outline is intended, we reiterate, only as a checklist or very rough guide. It makes no attempt to portray the sweep of developments in any of the regions and periods it embraces. The materials list, however, will provide the teacher with three types of assistance: first, reference works he may wish to consult for special preparation; second, written works, including anthologies of original writings, which he may wish to consider using in class, either instead of a textbook or as a supplement; and third, maps, films, and other teaching aids that may help illustrate the broad events of African history.

Forces, Themes, and Problems

**THE DEVELOPMENT
OF AGRICULTURE**

True history (as opposed to prehistory) invariably seems to follow the development of agriculture and a settled existence by a people. Through the cultivation of crops a surplus of production permits a division of labor, which in turn supports the growth of a class of rulers, technicians, scribes, merchants, priests, and soldiers. For a time it was believed that Egypt was the first society to practice agriculture, then the credit shifted to the Sumerians of the Tigris-Euphrates region, and then to the Anatolian Plateau.

A useful way to introduce the study of ancient history is to focus on the discovery or adoption of agriculture and to look at the growth in society that followed:

☐ How did Egypt acquire the knowledge of cultivation? Did other Africans acquire it from the Egyptians or discover it independently? How did knowledge of agriculture spread from the areas in which it first appeared?

☐ What crops were important? Which were indigenous to Africa? How did non-African crops come to be cultivated in Africa?

☐ How did reliance on agriculture change the ways of living in various societies?

THE AFRICAN IRON AGE

Although both the Egyptians and Nubians knew of iron from very early times (as did possibly North Africans and West Africans) it seems to have come into important use only after the Assyrian invasions of the seventh century B.C. Meroe was one of the great centers of mining and smelting. By 500–400 B.C. iron was being smelted in West Africa, and within a few centuries its use was widespread over most of the continent. Gradually iron tools and weapons replaced those of stone, wood, and bone. Iron became a valuable trade commodity in much of Africa. The spread of the Bantu-speaking peoples throughout Africa south of the equator seems to have been facilitated by their knowledge of mining, smelting, and working iron into weapons and tools.

In much of Africa the use of iron became common at roughly the same time as dependence upon agriculture. The history of Africa for over two thousand years thus can be seen as that of a people using iron and farming to settle new lands, increase their population and wealth, and build up increasingly complex states and political systems.

The importance of iron parallels that of agriculture.
☐ Why was iron so important? What were the advantages of iron tools over those made from other materials?
☐ How did the knowledge of mining, smelting, and forging spread in Africa?
☐ How did peoples regard the possession of iron and a knowledge of how to work it? (In many societies, only members of the royal clans were allowed to learn iron technology, and thus a king had a near-monopoly over the supply of iron in his kingdom.)

Although Africans (with the exception of those of the Nile Valley and North Africa) traditionally made few tools of other metals, such as copper, bronze, and tin, they knew how to mine and work them. In parts of Africa that are mineral-rich, archeologists have found thousands of ancient mine shafts where gold, copper, and tin were produced. As will be noted below, these metals were used more for trade, currency, and ornaments than for tools, yet their importance to Africa proved to be great.

THE IMPACT OF FOREIGN RELIGIOUS-CULTURAL SYSTEMS

Christianity. As Christianity spread in the first few centuries after Christ, Africa proved to be fertile ground for the new religion. Egypt, Nubia, Ethiopia, and North Africa were important centers of Christianity by the fifth century. (St. Augustine was a North African.) There are faint clues that Christianity may have had slight impact south of the Sahara.

The influence of Christian thought, and of the Greek, Roman, and Jewish ideas that accompanied its spread in Africa, was considerable. Yet following the Arab conquest during the seventh century, Christianity rapidly faded out, except in Egypt, Nubia, and Ethiopia. Today only Ethiopia maintains its long tradition of Christianity as a national faith. It is a minority faith in Muslim Egypt and had virtually disappeared in the Nubian area by 1600.

A study of Africa under the influence of early Christianity is both interesting and important, despite the fact it was replaced by Islam in most areas.

☐ What factors facilitated the receptiveness to Christianity in northern Africa?

☐ What were its influences on society, government, trade, and learning?

☐ Why did it decline so rapidly when Islam began to compete with it?

Islam. Although early Christianity was a force in northern Africa, it was largely overshadowed by Islam after the Arab conquest of 650–750 A.D. and the subsequent migrations of Arabs into Africa. In Africa north of the Sahara millions welcomed the new religion, and the indigenous Africans gradually blended into the dominant Arab culture. For several centuries Morocco, Tunisia, and Algeria enjoyed a prominence as great as any they had ever before known. Their cities became centers of Islamic civilization, producing poets, historians, philosophers, and scientists as well as wielding substantial power within the Islamic empire. North African and Arab merchants and travelers crossed the Sahara increasingly after the eighth century, helping to expand the trade that had long trickled across desert roads from oasis to oasis. From the profits of this trade great states arose south of the Sahara; Tekrur and Ghana were in full flower by the ninth century.

Although Islam was adopted only slowly south of the Sahara, it won its first converts among the nobility. By the eleventh century a number of West African kings had accepted the new faith; later it began to influence the patterns of government and the economic system. By the sixteenth century literacy in Arabic was widespread in western Africa among the leading commercial and noble classes.

Through Islam and the trans-Saharan trade, ideas flowed both ways across the Sahara. The great states of Ghana, Mali, Songhai, and Kanem-Bornu were part of the Islamic world, although they never lost their basic African character.

Islam and the Arab influence were also consequential along the Indian Ocean coast of eastern Africa, where centuries of trade and intermarriage produced the Swahili people and their unique civilization based on coastal trading cities.

The history of more than two thirds of Africa north of the equator cannot be understood without taking into account the impact of Islam. Students should be encouraged to examine the basic precepts of Islam, its traditions of science and philosophy, its ideas about government and administration, and the ways in which all these ideas played a role in shaping the great states and cultures of Africa north of the equator.

ENVIRONMENTAL INFLUENCES

The size and power of states in Africa were rooted in the productivity of the land. In general, the most influential African political developments occurred in the most productive localities, while in the poorer environments progress was slower. The teacher will have noted that the course balances suggested in the Introduction frequently include a few days of attention to African geography. No full understanding of Africa is possible without some sense of the character of the soils, rainfall, mineral products, topography, and crop production; these factors have had a major influence on the course of African history up to the present.

ROLE OF TRADE SYSTEMS

Sharing importance with environmental factors is the role of commercial systems in Africa. Research in the past fifty years has demonstrated the existence of several critically important long-distance trading systems into which flowed the goods of most of the African continent, to be exchanged for a variety of goods from the Arab world, India, and southern Europe. Change in Africa was constantly affected by the flow of goods and ideas through these great trading systems. In most of Africa, the power of rulers depended as much on their control of commerce as on the internal production of wealth in their kingdoms.

Attention should be focussed on six major trading systems:

The Nile Valley System. Goods flowed up and down the Nile from ancient times, binding Egypt and Nubia together economically and drawing into the Nile cultural-economic world most peoples living adjacent to the great river.

The Red Sea System. Goods flowed from Egypt, Nubia, and Ethiopia into Red Sea ports, there to be transported to Arabia, Persia, India, and China. Goods from these lands flowed into northeastern Africa in exchange. The Red Sea served to link the interior of northeastern Africa with the Mediterranean and Indian Ocean commercial systems of Europe and Asia. The history of Nubia and Ethiopia are inextricably linked to the Red Sea trading system.

The Indian Ocean System. From before the time of Christ, mariners transported goods and ideas in a great arc around the northern, western, and eastern littoral of the Indian Ocean, linking eastern Africa with Arabia, Persia, India, China, and Indonesia. Through this system a number of Indonesian crops made their way into Africa: the Asian yam, banana, plantain, coco-yam, and coconut. The Swahili civilization was built on the Indian Ocean trading system and helped link the inland regions of modern Rhodesia, Zambia, and Mozambique with the outside world, as ivory, gold, iron, and copper were exported from this mineral-rich part of the continent.

The Trans-Saharan System. Across several major desert trade routes flowed goods from sub-Saharan Africa, in exchange for goods produced in North Africa, Europe, and the Middle East. A large part of ancient Europe's gold derived from sub-Saharan Africa, and the export of gold for the import of salt was a fundamental part of the trans-Saharan system. The great states of the West African Sudan owed their power directly to their control of the trans-Saharan trade, while states as far away as the forest region sold and bought through the sudanic markets.

West African Regional Systems. The vast and productive lands of West Africa were linked to the trans-Saharan system, but they also developed other subsystems through which goods flowed both east and west and north and south.

A network of trade routes, originating before 1000 A.D., bound most of West Africa together into a highly complex commercial region.

Central African Trading Systems. A number of other regional trading systems helped to facilitate interchange among the Bantu-speaking peoples of the Congo basin, Angola, Zambia, Rhodesia, and adjacent areas. Less is known of the specific operations of these systems before the eighteenth century, yet they definitely played an essential role in the exchange of goods from which chiefs and kings gained wealth and power.

SUDANIC CIVILIZATION CONCEPT

Today it is recognized that the Negroid peoples of Africa may have a common origin and that their cultures stem from a long-distant ancestral past. Although their main areas of ancient concentration were in the central and southern Sahara and in the sudanic grasslands south of the Sahara, they were linked in little-understood ways to both Egypt and Nubia in antiquity. As they expanded in population, they gradually moved southward over a period of several millennia, eventually populating virtually all of Africa south of the Sahara.

Deeply rooted ideas about God, about life, about government, and about making a living accompanied this expansion. Thus, even the great cultural diversity of the peoples of Africa cannot totally obscure the wide prevalence of a basic concept of monotheism, a tendency to build states headed by a divine or semi-divine king, and a tradition of symbolic expression in the plastic arts.

Many historians and anthropologists are coming to recognize in this distribution of related culture traits a common civilization, often referred to as the Sudanic civilization, because of its apparent origin in the sudanic grasslands south of the Sahara. An examination of the areas of commonality and variation within this civilization provides a useful approach to the study of African history and cultures.

Students can develop considerable interest in such questions as:

☐ What are the common characteristics of the African kingship system? What factors tended to encourage its development in various parts of Africa and to discourage it in others?

☐ To what extent does the pharaonic system of ancient Egypt exemplify this basic African political concept? How might the concept have been diffused in ancient times?

Similar questions can be examined in the areas of African art and religion.

The use of iron and other metals and a wide distribution of common agricultural techniques and crops, both basic characteristics of the Sudanic civilization, are also good subjects for student inquiry.

BANTU ORIGINS AND MIGRATIONS

The Bantu-speaking peoples today inhabit almost all of Africa south of the equator and in several places extend north of the equator. Among the broad questions in African history are where they originated, how they spread, and how they adapted to a variety of new environments. Their languages and basic cultural traditions obviously link them with the sudanic peoples of West Africa, yet during more than two thousand years of migrations they have also evolved numerous new ideas and customs.

A consideration of the problems of Bantu origins and migrations provides a very helpful focus for understanding the dynamics of African history: the influence of the environment, changes resulting from close contact with different peoples, the effects of trade, the influence of Islam, and the effects of isolation from differing peoples.

PROCESS OF STATE FORMATION AND DEVELOPMENT

Although many African societies, including some that are otherwise culturally well-developed, existed with little or no centralized political authority, a certain kind of centralized state was predominant in African societies. Historians of Africa have inevitably concentrated their attention on states, empires, and the institution of kingship. Because of this, most treatments of African history become studies of the rise, influence, and decline of powerful states.

It has been noted in several places above that the agricultural and mineral productivity of an area, as well as control of commerce, determined where centralized states would arise, and to what level of power they might reach. A common, and very helpful, focus for the study of African history is an examination of the formation and growth of states.

☐ What were the economic factors responsible? What were the ethnic factors in state formation?

☐ How did the king and his associates gain control over surplus wealth and the profits of trade? To what extent was conflict between states an outcome of struggle to control production or trade?

☐ What were the relationships between the crown and the ordinary people?

☐ How were kings selected and removed from power? To what extent could democratic processes operate within centralized kingship states?

☐ How did powerful kings govern? How did they select their immediate subordinates, their provincial and district administrators, and their military lieutenants? How were their successors chosen?

☐ How did a state grow into an empire?

The literature is rich in this area, and several of the sources recommended in the materials list will aid the teacher in approaching a study of the state process both in general and in specific cases.

These seven broad forces, problems, and themes provide the most useful foci for studying African history. They do not exhaust the possibilities, of course, but they are generally agreed to be the most important and effective for understanding the African historical process. They should provide the teacher with a flexible but comprehensive set of guides that will lend purpose and direction.

3 African history II: developments during the contact with Europe

After the 1430s Portuguese ships pushed farther and farther south along the West African coast and set into motion a new set of forces that had been previously absent in African history: a new trade system along the Atlantic coastline, an insatiable market for African slaves, a large supply of new goods, and direct contacts between African societies and alien cultures.

Between about 1440 and 1870 these forces were concentrated along the African coasts (except in South Africa and Algeria), rarely extending more than a few score miles inland except on a few major rivers. In the interior most Africans had never seen a European and were affected only indirectly by the slowly growing African-European relationship along the coasts.

After the 1870s the situation changed rapidly and dramatically. Africa was divided into spheres of influence claimed by various European nations. During the period 1880–1910 European troops seized virtually all of Africa, translating the spheres of influence into colonies controlled by European force of arms.

For this reason—the slowly growing but ultimately cataclysmic influence of Europe on African history—it is convenient to treat African history after the fifteenth century as a period separate from earlier history. Yet a strong caution is necessary. The historical forces that had long shaped African history continued to operate right into the twentieth century; indeed, they continue to play a role, even after independence. There is an *African* history during the period of European influence, within which the effects of the European contact slowly but progressively became a shaping force. Treating African history after the European contact began as a separate unit is a convenience, but nothing more.

As in the previous chapter, this chapter will provide a brief outline, primarily chronological, which the teacher may use as a rough guide or checklist. Whether the course follows a chronological sequence, or whether it focuses on forces and problems, the second section of the chapter, in which several major forces are described, should be carefully considered by the teacher and woven into classroom discussion and student study.

OUTLINE:
1450 to the Present

A. The Portuguese Era
    As the fifteenth century dawned, Portugal was the first European maritime country to acquire the naval technology and the drive to launch a program of world exploration. The grand objectives were to find the riches (gold, gems, spices, silks, ivory) of Africa and the Indies, thus bypassing the Muslim middlemen of the southern Mediterranean, and to find military support in the long struggle against Islamic power. As part of this latter ob-

jective, the specific hope was to find the land of the legendary Prester John, reputably a powerful Christian king in Africa who was surrounded by Islamic nations.

1. Portuguese explorations around the African coastline. Consider reasons for the Portuguese efforts, what they found, their attitudes, and their reports of African peoples and kingdoms.
2. Patterns of trade (exports, imports, trading relations)
3. Areas of special Portuguese effort (Gold Coast, Benin, Kongo, the Swahili coastal cities)

B. Northern European Period after 1600

Late in the sixteenth century both Holland and England emerged as great powers, able to compete on a worldwide basis with the formerly dominant Spanish and Portuguese. The Dutch took the lead in Africa and the Indian Ocean regions, soon supplanting the Portuguese. Within decades, however, Britain began to compete with Holland in Africa, and France soon followed. By the end of the seventeenth century Denmark, Sweden, and Prussia had also begun to trade extensively with Africa, and Portugal was largely confined to its interests in Angola and Mozambique.

C. Relationship with Coastal Africa
1. Patterns of trade
2. European respect for African power and political integrity

D. The Slave Trade
1. Reasons (labor needs in Europe, Atlantic islands, and New World)
2. Patterns of growth in the trade
3. The triangular pattern (Africa–New World–Europe)

   g)   The Berlin Conference, 1883–1884
   h)   Armed conquest, 1884–1900
8.   African resistance
   a)   Wars of resistance: Algeria, Sudan, Ethiopia,
        Senegal, Asante, Hausaland, Congo, South Af-
        rica, Tanganyika
   b)   Uprisings: Sierra Leone, Nigeria, Congo, An-
        gola, South-West Africa, Tanganyika, Rho-
        desia-Zambia
G.   Colonial Rule
   1.   Patterns of rule by British, French, Germans, Bel-
        gians, Portuguese
   2.   Development of transportation, cash crops, new
        governments
   3.   African reactions: repressive control of dissent, sep-
        aratist religious movements, expansion of modern
        nationalism
   4.   Effects of World War I and World War II
H.   Growth of Nationalism and the New Africa
   1.   Decline of traditional political power
   2.   Growth of education
   3.   Urbanization and economic changes
   4.   Rise of new African leadership, 1920–1950
   5.   Pan-Africanism and nationalist movements
   6.   The surge to independence, 1950–1960

Forces, Themes, and Problems

Even a cursory perusal of the above terse outline of African
history between about 1450 and 1960 indicates that it becomes increasingly difficult to follow a primarily chronological approach. Forces of many kinds were at work in Africa,

shaping the course of events in various parts of the continent at varying rates. Thus it becomes imperative to help students focus on these forces; no real understanding of modern African history is possible otherwise. Here are six broad kinds of forces that have been of critical importance in Africa in the past few centuries.

SHIFTS IN POWER CENTERS

Prior to about 1500 African history inevitably dwells upon the major states and empires that grew to power in Egypt, Nubia, North Africa, Ethiopia, sudanic West Africa, and the Indian Ocean coast. All these derived a significant measure of their strength from their participation in the great trade systems itemized in the previous chapter. But two broad forces helped to shift the areas of power concentration in the period of modern African history.

Growth of Productivity and Population

Between about 1200 and 1500 the populations of several previously lesser developed regions expanded, creating the basis for new power centers. The forests of West Africa, the savannas of Bantu central Africa, and the interlacustrine region (the area between the Great Lakes) of East Africa were the chief cases in point. In all three areas the people gradually filled up most of the available land, increased their production of crops and minerals, and began to develop strong, centralized states similar to those developed earlier in the more northerly parts of the continent. The roots of these states lay in their own production and their own cultures, not primarily in trade or foreign influence from any source. The great Bantu states of the interlacustrine area—Bunyoro, Buganda, Burundi, Rwanda—seem to have had little trade contact with the outside world or even with other parts of Africa between 1200 and 1800, their period of greatest growth.

In the other two areas, the forests and savannas, trade seems to have played a role, but not the most critical one. The forest states of West Africa, such as the Akan kingdoms of Akwamu, Denkyira, and Asante and the states of Ife and Benin, were linked into a great regional trading system that in turn connected with the trans-Saharan system. Yet these forest kingdoms were on the far periphery and gained nothing like the great benefits of commerce that had helped create Ghana, Mali, Songhai, Kanem-Bornu, and the Hausa states.

In Central Africa the empire of Mwene Mutapa benefited greatly from its participation in the Swahili-Indian Ocean trade system, yet the farther west one moves in that region, the less critical trade seems to have been. Several very powerful states matured between about 1300 and 1700 in that region: Kongo, Luba, Lunda.

The point here is that African historical development was underway in many parts of Africa *before* the European contact, due to factors that had nothing to do with Europe. By the time the European trading system on the Atlantic Ocean coast of Africa matured in the sixteenth century, dozens of kingdoms had already formed, expanded, and achieved considerable power. They had begun to rival the great states of the sudanic interior in size, power, and achievement, quite independently of the European contact.

Influence of the European Trade

While these intra-African developments were already underway, the opportunity to trade with the Portuguese and later

European merchants added an important economic benefit to the states of western Africa. No longer were they on the far periphery of commercial networks; now they were at the very center of an important new system. Goods that had long flowed exclusively to the north, toward the sudanic market cities, now began to move south from an ever expanding region, toward new market centers on the Atlantic coast and in the immediate interior.

This was not an abrupt shift. Between 1500 and 1600 the Atlantic trade expanded slowly, and the trans-Saharan trade gradually declined. But by 1600 the shift in the balance of power was definite. Songhai had been shattered by a Moroccan invasion, and the once great centers of Jenne, Timbuktu, and Gao began to shrink. As they shrank, cities and states that could control the flow of goods to and from the Atlantic began to expand: the great Hausa cities of Kano and Katsina, the interior states of Oyo and Nupe, the small kingdoms of Dahomey, and the several Akan states. By 1700 sudanic West Africa was in a period of general depression, while the process of growth along the coasts, and a few hundred miles into the interior, continued unabated.

The trade with Europe was a major force in this shift in power, although it had not set it into motion. Gold, long produced in Guinea and Asante for the sudanic markets, now could be traded at points all along the Atlantic coast with no middlemen to skim off customs duties and taxes. In exchange the Africans received European muskets, iron tools, cloth, nails, rope, and hundreds of other valued products. (Most of these products were already known; either they were produced by African craftsmen or were imported from the sudanic markets. But they were expensive, until the abundant quantities brought in European ships helped to lower prices substantially.) Europeans came to refer to areas of West Africa by the names of the goods they could trade for: the Pepper Coast around Liberia, the Ivory Coast, the Gold Coast, the Slave Coast, and the Oil Rivers (the delta of the Niger was known for its palm oil).

EFFECTS OF THE ATLANTIC TRADE

Cheaper Imported Goods

As just noted, European ships could deliver a variety of manufactured goods to coastal Africa at lower prices than had been previously possible. A bolt of silk or cotton could be bought for, say, an ounce of gold; previously the bolt had been brought by camel across the Sahara, by donkey along the savannas, and by human bearers into the rain forests, with profits accruing to middlemen all along the way. Its final cost might have been three or four times as high.

The new flow of cheaper goods meant that kings, merchants, and noblemen could obtain large quantities of highly prized goods, since they monopolized the export of African goods and the import of European merchandise. A king could surround himself with lavish displays of wealth to demonstrate his stature. He could provide large rewards to his servants, assistants, vassals, and soldiers in return for their loyal service. This in turn meant he could support larger courts, a more extensive bureaucracy, and a larger body of soldiers. His power was thus measurably increased, so that he could expand his kingdom and exercise control over a larger and more prosperous state.

The new flow of goods did not produce a wide, popular demand; most were still too expensive for the average person. But for those individuals in the service of the state or engaged in commerce, new tastes and incentives resulted from the availability of goods through the European trade.

Depression of African Industry

The larger, cheaper flow of manufactured goods from Europe had a distinctly negative effect on African industry. As a general rule the goods brought in European ships came from areas (in Europe, India, or the New World) where they were produced more efficiently than Africans could produce them. Thus some of the most fundamental technological achievements of Africa were dealt a crippling blow by the competition. African iron-working, especially in those areas that had meager ore resources, became a rare kind of industry. Weaving, long known in most parts of Africa, virtually disappeared in the face of competition with cheap cottons from Europe and Asia.

Just as the African–European trade grew slowly, so the deterioration of African handicraft industries occurred gradually. The first effects were naturally on and near the coasts where European goods appeared in greatest quantities. But over a period of several centuries, the negative effects on African technology spread through much of the continent. By the time of the colonial conquest, at the end of the nineteenth century, many African societies were less highly developed in the material sense than they had been before the European contact began.

Spread of Firearms

Those states that had the closest contact with European traders soon began to buy muskets, powder, and shot. Continued growth of power for many African states was due, in part, to their possession of firearms. The introduction of firearms on a large scale was an important factor in the shifting balances of power in many parts of the continent.

It is useful to note that firearm sales to Africa consisted of inferior or obsolete weapons, so that at no time were Africans as effectively armed as Europeans of the same period.

EFFECTS OF THE SLAVE TRADE

On African Politics

Since trade with Europe clearly enriched and increased the power of those kings most involved, it is clear that the slave trade had the same effect. By the early eighteenth century the trade in slaves was the most important component of the African–European trade, overshadowing any other African export. There is no doubt that many African states were able to expand their power because they captured and exported slaves, just as there is no doubt that many African societies were injured because a great number of their people were sold into slavery. As a general rule, highly organized states profited, while decentralized societies suffered.

This is a problem over which both popular and scholarly controversy has raged. Some have exaggerated the effect of the slave trade, arguing that many African kings grew to power solely on the basis of slave exports, while others were virtually destroyed. Others have insisted that the slave trade had no real economic or political effect on Africa. This topic easily arouses student interest because of the emotional re-action to the slave trade. Focus on such questions as these:

☐ Which states benefited from the slave trade? Which suffered?

☐ To what extent did states engage in wars to capture slaves for the trade?

☐ How much of the wealth of slave-trading states derived from the sale of slaves compared to internal production and the sale of goods?

On African Populations

Did African populations decline because of the slave trade? Controversy has also characterized efforts to answer this question. Some writers have asserted that the slave trade removed somewhere between 25,000,000 and 70,000,000 Africans from their homes between about 1450 and 1870. They argue that this massive removal of people served to depopulate large parts of Africa; one estimate states that Africans comprised about one fifth of the world's population in 1600, but now comprise about one twelfth, and it assigns the chief responsibility for the loss of population to the slave trade.

Others argue that removal into slavery helped check accelerating population increases, which might soon have overpopulated the African land. They point out that West Africa, the area hardest hit by slaving, is today the most densely populated and prosperous large region of the continent.

Most authorities agree that two areas, Angola and Tanganyika, did indeed suffer depopulation as a result of slaving.

The most authoritative estimates of the volume of the slave trade indicate that it was slightly less than was once believed; the Atlantic trade landed around 9,500,000 slaves in Europe and the New World. When estimates of slave mortality on the Atlantic crossing and deaths due to slave raids, starvation, and ill treatment are added, this figure can be doubled to some 20,000,000 Africans having died or been taken from Africa during the four centuries of the Atlantic slave trade. Another 3,000,000 to 4,000,000 can be added to this figure for the Indian Ocean trade, as well as another

1,000,000 (a guess) for the long-time trade in slaves across the Sahara.

Such a vast removal of human beings, even over a period of centuries, must have had some effect on population—whether large areas were substantially reduced in population or merely grew more slowly than they would otherwise have done.

On Attitudes and Values

The figures above give a quantitative suggestion of the enormity of the African slave trade, but they cannot convey the ethical consequences of slavery. Perhaps, if so many Africans had been killed outright, history might have gradually diluted any sense of burning injustice for the crime. But with tens of millions of the descendants of enslaved Africans living today in the New World, history cannot erase or erode their testament to the inhumaneness of the slave trade.

The racial prejudices and mistrust that today characterize relations between Blacks and Whites in North America and Europe stem from the slave trade. In a fundamental sense, Europeans were unable to resolve the moral conflict between their values of human dignity and the squalid realities of their enslavement of Africans—except by constructing a myth that portrayed the African as something less than human. For centuries Europeans who trafficked in slaves, or owned them, continued to embellish this complex myth to ameliorate their sense of wrongdoing. European superiority was constantly considered to be natural and God-given; Africans were by nature inferior. Africans lived an animalistic, brutalized life in Africa, compared to which slavery was an improvement. Africans had none of the finer sentiments, were incapable of love, did not understand such qualities as mercy, and were inhumane to each other.

Americans are intimately aware of the blunter forms of this racist myth, which is under sustained attack within the American culture. But even as we gradually free ourselves from the more obvious errors of the myth, we retain (as do most Europeans) its legacy in our attitudes about Africa. This myth denigrated virtually every aspect of African culture, even the African land, in order to make Africa seem as harsh, unpleasant, and barbaric as possible. Thus Africa has been described as hot, humid, disease-ridden, dark, and dangerous—the slave traders were virtually delivering poor Africans from a living hell by selling them in the New World. Africans were characterized as people without culture and without history. Their minds were thought to be filled with rank superstitions and fears. Their kings were portrayed as brutal, savage tyrants who tortured and killed their subjects capriciously, and sold their own people into slavery for profit. (Rarely were people sold by their own rulers, and then only when they had committed crimes.)

Thus the development of racism and the myths of African inferiority are possibly the most serious effects of the slave trade, because they are still alive in the unconscious minds of most Europeans and Americans; they subtly affect relationships even in the 1970s. They have left a legacy of deep bitterness in the minds of the descendants of enslaved Africans as well as many modern Africans in Africa, who see the slave period as a monstrous mistreatment of Black by White.

As will be noted below, the myth of African inferiority was amplified during the European conquest and colonial period.

Teachers will find this topic of interest to many students,

and it has considerable relevance to the study of modern American race relations as well as to African study. Several sources cited in the materials list provide teacher or students with fascinating documentary help in tracing the origins and development of the myths of African inferiority.

FORCES AT WORK DURING COLONIAL RULE

No one force or period in the history of Africa can compare in effect with the period of colonial rule. In a space of no more than eighty years (1880–1960) almost the entire continent was entered by foreign troops, conquered, placed under new forms of rule, required to adhere to an alien pattern of law and administration, pressed into service in a European-dominated world economy, and exposed to accelerated culture change under foreign direction. Naturally the traditional fabric of African life resisted complete change and destruction, and the ancient forces of change in Africa continued to operate. But a new set of forces, powerful in nature and intensely concentrated in time, changed some of the directions of African development abruptly.

New Economic Forces

The fundamental reason for the colonial conquest was economic; Europe wanted secure sources of raw materials and a ready market for its burgeoning industrial production. Almost the first action taken after military conquest was to construct railroads, roads, and ports, all designed to open up the African interior to exploitation. Colonial governments undertook programs of development that were largely dictated by the economic needs of their home countries. If wild rubber was needed (as in the case of King Leopold's Congo), then a comprehensive effort was launched to obtain it. Transportation facilities to rubber-producing areas were opened; concessions were granted to European companies to exploit the rubber; Africans were required by law to work in the concessions and to produce more rubber; noncooperation by Africans was severely punished.

Some of the harshest events of the imposed colonial rule arose from the enforcement of new economic patterns. In the Congo, in a period of less than thirty years as many as 3,000,000 Congolese died as a result of punitive actions by Leopold's administrators and commercial concessionaires when Africans attempted to resist being pressed into the economic service of Leopold's state. In the bloody Maji-Maji rebellion in German Tanganyika, more than 100,000 Africans died when they resisted German efforts to force them to grow cotton instead of their traditional subsistence crops.

Taxes were almost universally levied on African men or villages, partly to support the cost of colonial rule and partly to force them to grow the cash crops needed by European industrialists and merchants.

As a result of these new economic forces, major changes occurred in African economic life: taxation and the need for cash were introduced, millions of men were forced to sell their labor, new crops were introduced and expanded, and labor was diverted from traditional pursuits into mining, cash agriculture, plantations, work on roads and railroads, and urban occupations. For better or worse, the result introduced irreversible changes in African economic life and aroused popular tastes for new goods, education, and urban living.

Social Changes

Both the physical presence of Europeans and the changes in economic patterns accelerated changes in African social life. Roads facilitated communication among peoples of differing ethnic origin; towns and cities built on European lines introduced an alternative to traditional life. Men who worked on plantations, road gangs, mines, or urban jobs either left their families for long periods or uprooted their families to move into a new social environment. The spread of Western education resulted in changed social ideas and values of schooled Africans and served to alter the status of women as girls began attending schools.

Political Changes

Critically important changes in the way in which Africans were governed followed colonial rule. The power of kings and chiefs was almost universally eroded, so that ordinary Africans were forced to look to different institutions for leadership. These institutions tended to be either the colonial government or the expanding class of educated, urbanized Africans who had learned European ways, values, and political techniques.

Whether colonial governments practiced direct rule or ruled indirectly through hereditary or appointed chiefs, the ultimate effect was to weaken the institution of chieftainship. Even under indirect rule, Africans came to realize that real power stemmed from the colonial administration, which set limits within which chiefs could rule; chiefs who stepped outside these limits were removed and replaced by more compliant appointees. By the time of the new African nationalism, in the 1940s and 1950s, chiefs in most of Africa had become politically impotent figureheads. Generally their office was respected by their people, but largely for reasons of custom and tradition rather than for power.

Changes in Values

A fascinating area of study is the changes in African values that took place under colonial rule. In the past few years it has become clear that the majority of Africans, including those who continue to live in rural areas, apparently in a traditional way, have embraced values of material and political progress with considerable eagerness.

Sometimes this popular change in values is referred to as "the revolution of rising expectations" because its most forceful expression lies in the realm of material progress. But the expectations of tens of millions of Africans extend far beyond the material realm; they aspire to a total transformation in African societies and conditions that will put them on equal terms with Europe and the world. Africans are widely aware of the fact that they have lagged behind much of the world, and they are eager to catch up.

The change in values began in many parts of Africa before European conquest, but colonial rule helped to speed it along. One reason for the massive popular support given to the new nationalist leaders during the 1950s and 1960s was the adoption of new values by much of the population. These same values account for the contemporary expectation that leaders must either produce tangible progress or be replaced by other leaders who may do better; this will be one of the major themes discussed in later chapters. In a classroom study of the colonial period, however, it is very helpful to direct student attention to the processes at work during the colonial period that helped to introduce Western values in so much of Africa.

AFRICAN REACTIONS TO CONQUEST
AND COLONIAL RULE

If we accept the dictum that a major objective of historical study is to help one understand the present, consideration of the African reaction to colonial conquest and rule is an excellent demonstration of the value of history. Part of the myth developed to justify colonialism was the assertion that Africans were constantly at war with each other and generally welcomed European rule in order to live in peace. Because of this belief, most Europeans and Americans doubted that the African people would support demands for independence with much enthusiasm when these demands were voiced by nationalist leaders of the 1940s and 1950s. Much research has been done in the past few years on the African reaction to colonialism, and the picture that emerges is of energetic resistance and frequent attempts to defy colonial rule.

An understanding of the extent and nature of the African resistance helps us to understand better the modern African suspiciousness of foreign influence and their vigilance against possible interference. Africans quickly became aware that Europe meant to impose its rule and its ways, and they fought doggedly, against impossible odds, to retain their independence.

American students find this aspect of the colonial period of special interest. Teachers are urged to direct student attention to it with such questions as the following:

☐ What were the major wars of resistance?
☐ What factors accounted for European successes?
☐ How did the ordinary people of Africa react to conquest?
What forms of resistance were used during the colonial pe-

riod itself, when armed struggle and political opposition were impossible?

NATIONALISM AND PAN-AFRICANISM

The driving political force that brought African nations to independence and provided a cohesive sense of purpose was African nationalism, which in turn is linked historically with the concept of Pan-Africanism, or the unity of Africans against outside domination. Both concepts were formulated during the colonial period by Africans who were well educated, often in close cooperation with politically conscious intellectuals of the "African Diaspora"—Black individuals from the United States and the West Indies. Even in Southern Africa, where Europeans continue to rule large African majorities, these sentiments have served to unify African resentment toward Whites. Students will find it profitable to consider the close links between early American civil rights leaders, such as W.E.B. Du Bois, and the leaders of the independence movements of Ghana, Nigeria, Kenya, and many other African nations.

African nationalism embraces ideas of self-determination, of freedom from foreign influence, of rapid economic modernization, of cooperation among African nations, of state-dominated economic development, and of neutralism in world ideological contentions. Although the form of nationalism differs from country to country, most African leaders continue to espouse its basic principles. (In later chapters it will be pointed out that new national ideologies are beginning to amend the historic nationalist concepts of the colonial and early independent periods.)

Although African nationalism has had many positive tenets, some of its most compelling ideas have had a negative quality: rejecting alien domination, combatting inequalities between Africa and Europe, which helped the process of slavery and colonial conquest, and protesting against neo-colonialism and economic disadvantages.

These negative tenets were essential during the colonial period, since the overwhelming task facing Africa was free-ing itself from outside rule. In view of the vast changes that occurred in African life during the colonial period, African spokesmen recognized that no pre-European ideologies or political concepts fitted the needs of twentieth-century Af-rica. Their objective was to gain power, so that Africa could begin to formulate its new ideas and self-images in the process of entering the modern world on an equal footing.

Teaching Materials

During the past fifteen years there has been an enormous increase in published African historical studies, and many of the new books help to rectify the biases and errors that plagued earlier works on Africa's history. Any teacher faced with the scores of available books will have difficulty select-ing the more helpful ones, unless he is that rare person who is a specialist in African history.

The first part of this section lists a number of books that are generally sound, even though the average teacher will not have time to use more than a few. This selection is in-tended to help the teacher evaluate books to which she may have access, and to recommend a basic library of books on African history for those schools that may wish to build up a good (although not too costly) reference collection for use by both teachers and students. The annotations are designed to help the teacher choose only a few titles when time or budget limit more extensive reading or acquisitions.

GENERAL SUMMARIES FOR ALL AFRICA

Africa in History. Basil Davidson. A good general history that combines chronology with an analysis of themes and forces. Easy reading, slightly flowery, offers a persuasive argument in favor of African achievements. Macmillan Company, 866 Third Ave., New York, N.Y. 10017. 1969. $6.95.

Africa to 1875. Robin Hallett. A good, scholarly summary, but only up to the colonial conquest. Strongest where European contacts and Islam are concerned. Readable. University of Michigan Press, Ann Arbor, Mich. 48106. 1968. $8.50.

History of African Civilization. E. Jefferson Murphy. A sound, well-written general summary of all phases of African history. Contains considerable material drawn from anthropology, archaeology, and linguistics, presented clearly. Thomas Y. Crowell, 201 Park Ave. South, New York, N.Y. 10003. 1972. $12.50.

Horizon History of Africa. The most lavish and costly book on African history, with chapters written by eminent scholars. Abundant illustrations and many quotations from original writings, legends, and documents. American Heritage Publishing Company, 551 Fifth Ave., New York, N.Y. 10017. 1971. $25.

Problems in African History, 4th ed., 2 vols. Robert Collins, ed. Organized around a variety of themes, the books bring together valuable and often difficult to obtain primary resource materials. Collins, a professor at the University of California, Santa Barbara, introduces each theme and places each reading in an understandable context. Problem seven treats the African slave trade. Produced for the undergraduate market and recommended for library purchase for senior high schools. Prentice-Hall, Englewood Cliffs, N.J. 07632. 1972. $5.95. pap.

BOOKS ON PORTIONS OF AFRICAN HISTORY

Africa in the Nineteenth and Twentieth Centuries. Joseph C. Anene and Godfrey Brown, eds. 1964. $5.
A Thousand Years of West African History. J.F. Ade Ajayi and Ian Espie, eds. 1964. $5.50.
Both of these titles were written by African university academics. They represent research efforts up to 1964. Teachers of history at the secondary level in African schools were faced with new curricular demands. Their training had not usually included formal work in African history, and many felt a need for a pair of texts that would orient thinking and chart the way to more detailed sources. If American educators choose an historical approach as part of their study of Africa, these volumes may have a similar value. Depending upon reading levels and the grade level at which the historical approach is to be used, these titles may also be of some benefit to students. They can be of assistance to teachers. Humanities Press, Inc., 450 Park Avenue South, New York, N.Y. 10010.
Ancient Africa. F.A. Chijioke. Recommended for junior high use. Used in upper elementary grades in Nigeria.

Colorful and effective illustrations. Africana Publishing Company, 101 Fifth Ave., New York, N.Y. 10003. 1967. $2.40.

Christians and Muslims in Africa. Noel King. Concise historical survey with bibliography for general reader. Harper and Row, 10 East 53 St., New York, N.Y. 10022. 1971. $4.50.

East Africa Through a Thousand Years, A.D. 1000 to the Present Day. G.S. Were (University of Nairobi, History Department) and D.A. Wilson. This text is used in East African secondary schools and is recommended. Africana Publishing Company, 101 Fifth Ave., New York, N.Y. 10003. 1968. $4.95.

East and Central Africa to the Late Nineteenth Century. Basil Davidson and J. Mhina. Chapters 21 and 22 offer a cultural approach to life in Central Africa before the coming of European influences. Doubleday Anchor original, Garden City, N.Y. 11530. 1969. $1.95, pap.

The History of Africa in Maps, rev. ed. Harry A. Gailey, Jr. A novel approach to the subject. Best used in the library or as a teacher reference. Classroom use for inductive teaching via map analysis is also possible. Denoyer-Geppert Company, 5235 Ravenswood Ave., Chicago, Ill. 60640. 1972. $2.50, pap.

A History of West Africa. J.D. Fage. This is a revised edition of an earlier work. Concisely written, the British author does begin to reflect newer African interpretations of themes and events. The book is recommended as an introduction to the history of the region as viewed by a non-African scholar long familiar with the region. Cambridge University Press, 32 East 57 St., New York, N.Y. 10022. 1971. $1.95.

A History of West Africa to the Nineteenth Century. Basil
Davidson with F.K. Buah and J.F. Ade Ajayi. This book
is used by African secondary school students. It combines a number of approaches to the study of history.
Chapters 12–14 may be useful for a cultural approach.
Doubleday Anchor original, Garden City, N.Y. 11530.
1968. $1.95, pap.

The Maghreb in the Modern World. Samir Amin. An introduction to the modern economics of Morocco, Algeria,
and Tunisia. Provides brief historical analysis of colonial
impact before concentrating on contemporary economic
and social change. Amin brings a Third World view to
his subject without rigidly using deterministic philosophy. Penguin Books, 7110 Ambassador Rd., Baltimore,
Md. 21207. 1970. $2.25. pap.

Pictorial History of Ethiopia. R. Pankhurst. A pictorial description of 2,500 years of Ethiopian history. Useful
library addition. Oxford University Press, 200 Madison
Ave., New York, N.Y. 10022. 1969. $2.

Prehistory of Africa. J.D. Clark. A concise synthesis, excellent time line, and culture succession maps. Highly
recommended. Praeger Publishers, 111 Fourth Ave.,
New York, N.Y. 10003. 1971. $8.50.

Tarikh. A semi-annual Nigerian-produced journal of history
aimed at upper secondary level students and teachers
throughout English-speaking Africa. Humanities Press,
450 Park Ave. South, New York, N.Y. 10001. $3, for two
issues.

Zamini, a Survey of East African History. This book is used
in East African secondary schools and is recommended
for teacher use. Africana Publishing Company, 101
Fifth Ave., New York, N.Y. 10003. 1968. $3.80.

Slave Trade of Africa

The following is a short list of recommended reading materials for teachers whose various courses touch upon the slave trades of Africa. There were three distinct such trades: Trans-Atlantic, Trans-Saharan, and Western Indian Ocean. One or two of these areas may be covered in such courses as United States history, world history, or various studies of Africa.

Africa Remembered. Philip Curtin, ed. Narratives by West Africans from the era of the slave trade. University of Wisconsin Press, Box 1379, Madison, Wis. 53701. 1968. $2.95.

Atlantic Slave Trade: Pre-Colonial History 1450–1850. (Original title *Black Mother.*) Basil Davidson. Survey of the trans-Atlantic slave trade. Useful study for the general reader with special emphasis on European methods of organizing the slave trade. Atlantic-Little, Brown, 34 Beacon St., Boston, Mass. 02106. 1964. $2.45.

Black Cargoes. Daniel Mannix and Malcolm Cowley. A history of the Atlantic slave trade. Viking Press, 625 Madison Ave., New York, N.Y. 10022. 1965. $1.85, pap.

The Dimensions of the Atlantic Slave Trade. Philip Curtin. Using a statistical and documents approach the author, a professor of history at the University of Wisconsin, offers convincing evidence on the actual numbers of Africans enslaved and removed to the New World. The final chapters analyze and speculate on the impact of the slave trade on West African society. Recommended for teachers of American and African history. University of Wisconsin Press, Box 1379, Madison, Wis. 53701. 1971. $7.95.

Equiano's Travels. Paul Edwards, ed. One of the few

English accounts by an African who was enslaved.
Praeger Publishers, 111 Fourth Ave., New York, N.Y.
10003. 1967. $4.95.

The Fortunate Slave. Douglas Grant. An example of African
slavery in the early eighteenth century. Story of a
Gambian who was enslaved and taken to Maryland.
Oxford University Press, 200 Madison Ave., New York,
N.Y. 10016. 1968. $7.50.

Colonialism and Nationalism

Africa Since 1800. R. Oliver and A. Atmore. A survey approach that is strongest for former English colonial
regions. Useful introductory bibliography. Cambridge
University Press, 3 East 57 St., New York, N.Y. 10019.
1967. $1.95.

Child of Two Worlds. Mugo Gatheru. Mr. Gatheru's account
of his youth in Kenya and encounters with European
settlers provides a sensitive insight into the colonial
system. His experiences in the United States are also
recounted. Doubleday Anchor original, Garden City,
N.Y. 11530. 1965. $1.25. pap.

Not Yet Uhuru. Oginga Odinga. Autobiography of the
Kenyan Nationalist leader, particularly useful for insights into the colonial education system and its impact
on local culture. Hill and Wang, Inc., 72 Fifth Ave.,
New York, N.Y. 10011. 1967. $2.45.

AUDIO-VISUAL MATERIALS

Record for Teacher Background

Africa and the Origin of Man. Basil Davidson. A prelude to
the study of African history with study guide and intro-

duction by J.H. Clarke. AMIE Associates, Inc., 123 Manhattan Ave., New York, N.Y. 10027, or J.H. Clarke, Department of Black and Puerto Rican Studies, Hunter College, Park Ave. and 68th. St., New York, N.Y. 10019. $7.95.

Wall Charts

D.C.A. Educational Products, Inc., 4065 Stenton Ave., Philadelphia, Pa. 19144. *Ethiopia Picture Set*. Range in size from 8½" × 11" to 17" × 24". Twelve charts in set. Historical survey using drawings and photographs for wall display or visual teaching tool. Highly recommended. $3.50. Another picture packet is *Songhai and Benin*. Pictures with comment on early West African political systems. $3.50.

Social Studies School Services, 10,000 Culver Blvd., Culver City, Calif. 90230. *African Heritage, Great West African Civilizations*. Large wall chart 30" × 40" with teaching notes. Highly recommended. $1.95. *Anglo-Boer War, 1899–1902*. Useful as wall display or individual study unit. 10" × 14". $5. *Slave Trade and Its Abolition*. A collection of contemporary documents. 10" × 14" study packet. U.K. product distributed in the U.S. $5.

Transparencies

African History and Culture. Two parts, twenty transparencies, sixty-two overlays. Aevec Inc., 500 Fifth Ave., New York, N.Y. 10019. $115.

Sub-Saharan Africa. Eleven themes each with four to eight overlays. Both sources recommended for examination. Keuffel and Esser Company, 300 Adams St., Hoboken, N.J. 07030. Prices range from $3.25–$9.25.

Films and Filmstrips

Unfortunately very few accurate or technically strong films or filmstrips currently exist.

The Ancient Africans. 27 min., color, 1970. Highly recommended for preview as a survey film. The International Film Foundation. $325.

Proud Heritage from West Africa. Two strips with record. One strip on grassland kingdoms of Ghana, Mali, and Songhai; one strip concentrates on forest states of Oyo, Benin, and Ashanti. Guidance Associates. $37.50.

PROFESSIONAL JOURNALS

International Journal of African History. Africana Publishing Company, 101 Fifth Ave., New York, N.Y. 10003. Quarterly, $15 for individuals; $20 for institutions.

Journal of African History. Cambridge University Press, 3 East 57 St., New York, N.Y. 10022. Quarterly, $17.50.

4 Nation building in Africa I: national, political, and economic development

The study of African geography and history is important, and most schools that include Africa in the curriculum require at least some attention to it. It is equally important, however, to include a study of modern Africa. Most students, even those who find geography and history interesting, are interested in Africa today and want to achieve a better understanding of events and problems in the new nations of contemporary Africa.

This chapter and the following one focus on contemporary Africa. Although they deal with rather different content, they are linked with each other by the concept of "nation building." This concept, which is defined below, is a useful and meaningful way to approach an understanding of contemporary Africa, because it emphasizes the dynamic processes of experimentation, problem solving, and development that are absorbing the energies and thoughts of most modern Africans.

What Nation Building Is

The narrowest definition of nation building is the process of creating a sense of national loyalty and identification among a population that has traditionally been divided into numerous tribes, ethnic groups, or smaller political units. The term is often used in studying or analyzing modern Africa, Asia, and Latin America, but it is most frequently used in the study of Africa. The fact that the colonial powers divided Africa into roughly fifty new political territories, most of which had not previously existed, and that these territories have achieved independence as sovereign nations during the past twenty years, make it clear that nation building is a process of fundamental importance in Africa.

If the concept of nation building is to be employed as a framework for studying modern Africa, its definition must be broadened to include a variety of political, economic, social, and cultural forces that are inseparable from the process of building a sense of national identity. In this chapter, as well as the following chapter, the concept of nation building includes the following elements.

NATIONAL POLITICAL STRUCTURE

A nation must have a structure of government, both national and local, which can effectively unite the people of the country. It must have a constitution, written or unwritten (in African nations the constitutions are always written), a head of government, and some form of congress or parliament that provides for the representation of the diverse ethnic, economic, sectional, and political interests in the country.

The government must be structured in a way to provide the administrative services required for modern living: taxation, social services, elections, defense, foreign relations, justice, maintenance of internal security, commerce, communication, education, and resolution of conflict.

Every African government is organized to furnish these essential functions, at least on paper. But developing the many needed agencies and institutions into effective instruments began, in a sense, only when each nation achieved independence and is still very much in progress.

NATIONAL IDENTITY

Since many of the new nations of Africa took shape only during the colonial period, in the late nineteenth or early twentieth century, a high priority has been to foster an attitude on the part of the people that is national, rather than tribal or local. In recent years the world has pointed repeatedly to the fact that Africans have traditionally been divided into more than eight hundred ethnic groups or "tribes." It is widely believed that the average African thinks of himself, first and foremost, as a member of his tribe rather than of his nation. In Ghana, for example, this view holds that the average person thinks of himself as a Ga, an Asante, a Fante, a Dagomba, or a member of one or another smaller ethnic group and is often only vaguely aware that he lives in a country that has adopted the name Ghana.

There is substance to this belief, although it is generally exaggerated and misinterpreted, as will be discussed later. The leaders of every nation in Africa have given high priority to persuading their citizens to think of themselves as Ghanaians, Kenyans, Nigerians, Senegalese, Tunisians, or Zambians rather than in ethnic terms. In most African nations, an accusation of "tribalism" against an individual or a

Africa in 1972

group is as invidious as an accusation of "racism" against an American.

African nations use a variety of techniques to foster national loyalty and identity: flags, anthems, art programs, national dance movements, political oratory, school programs, national youth and citizen organizations and patriotic movements, special radio and television broadcasts, and even laws prohibiting tribal alliances or political parties.

NATIONAL ECONOMIC DEVELOPMENT

The third aspect of nation building is the broad process of expanding and improving the wealth of the nation and its people. Virtually all of Africa is underdeveloped economically, and Africans are deeply dissatisfied with poverty, gradual progress, and shortages of goods. Every African leader has recognized that his nation cannot be built unless there is accelerated and tangible economic development.

At the end of the colonial period almost every African nation was in a condition of poverty. Most people grew only enough food to sustain themselves and their families and to buy the barest minimum of goods. There were few industries; almost all manufactured goods had to be imported at high cost. Railroads, roads, waterways, and airlines connected only the major centers, leaving many of the rural areas isolated, with no easy way to ship goods to market. Mineral resources were untapped, often unknown. Power was in short supply. And the economy tended to be based on the production of one crop or one mineral ore, or a very few at best.

Independence, to the peoples of each African nation, meant deliverance from underdevelopment as well as political freedom from alien rule. They have insisted that the process of nation building include material and economic progress and that this progress be rapid. Where governments have failed to show rapid progress, popular dissent has arisen, and many governments have fallen; old leaders have been replaced with new ones who promise to accelerate the pace of economic development.

SOCIAL AND CULTURAL DEVELOPMENT

Although this extensive and vital area is the subject of the next chapter, it is essential to note here that it must be considered part of the nation-building process. Nation building involves large shifts of population, especially from rural areas to the burgeoning urban areas. It involves changes in social values and attitudes. It is linked with changes in individual aspirations and ambitions, the outlook of youth, the ties of the family, the position of women, the relation between the individual and the state, the expansion of education, and many other changes in social life in African nations.

STUDY OF MODERN AFRICA THROUGH THE FRAMEWORK OF NATION BUILDING

The teacher will have perceived in this brief discussion of nation building that it is a vast, complex area of study. If the framework is to facilitate student understanding of contemporary Africa, it must be well organized. The remainder of this chapter will be devoted to providing a sufficiently organized and specific framework; the chief facets, elements, principles, and forces that affect nation building will be listed and briefly described.

A major problem facing the teacher is how to apply this framework in a way that will stimulate and guide students to a real understanding of the processes at work in Africa today. It will be recognized immediately that no teacher could attempt to lead a class through the nation-building process of every African country, even though similar principles of nation building are at work throughout the continent. For this reason it is strongly recommended that a class focus on a very limited number of countries, preferably from two to five. In selecting these countries the teacher should use several criteria:

☐ Materials on the countries selected should be readily available and suitable for the class level. (The section on materials will help in determining this.)

☐ The countries selected should preferably be contrasting, along some of the following lines:

Size. At least one large and one small.

Location. East, west, north, south, center. Non-independent countries are not recommended; the process of nation building is complicated by colonial or minority-rule factors. These countries are treated in Chapter Eight: Angola, Mozambique, Rhodesia, South Africa, South-West Africa (Namibia), and Guinea (Bissau).

Wealth. At least one that is better developed or possessing significant known resources, another with poorer assets.

Colonial legacy. Preferably contrasting according to its colonial heritage, e.g., British, French, Belgian, or non-colonial (Ethiopia, Liberia, Egypt).

Several suggested groups of countries, for which there are

ample materials, are listed below. The teacher is urged, however, to feel free to choose others to vary these, especially if special resources are available: if the teacher has special knowledge, if students have visited one or another country, or if there are accessible to the school nationals from an African country or Americans who have lived in Africa.

Sample country groupings are:
Ghana, Malawi, Somalia
Ivory Coast, Liberia, Uganda
Kenya, Zambia, Senegal
Togo, Kenya, Ethiopia
Nigeria, Zambia, Botswana
Zaire, Tanzania, Dahomey
Ghana, Tanzania, Zaire
Morocco, Sierra Leone, Zambia

The Framework of Nation Building

GOVERNMENT AND POLITICS

The Colonial Legacy

Every African nation (except Egypt, Ethiopia, and Liberia) became independent with a structure of government and politics that was based on the pattern set during the colonial period, although in every case modifications were made at the time of independence, and in many cases further modifications have been made subsequently.

The colonial pattern tended to be one with a Governor or Governor-General (whose office became that of President or Prime Minister), with an assembly that had limited powers;

the assembly was usually partially elected and partially appointed. Upon independence the assembly became the chief legislative body (Assembly in the French areas, Parliament in the British), and it was composed of popularly elected members. Each colonial territory had a civil administration, operating under the Governor, which included provincial, district, and urban administrators. Upon independence this structure (with African administrators replacing those of European origin) became a department of local administration, under the supervision of an elected minister (usually the Minister of Local Government). Only rarely has the local administration been modified to operate through elected administrators; most are salaried, appointed civil servants. The strong central authority of the colonial era, in other words, has been continued or even strengthened under African rule since independence.

National level politics was virtually nonexistent during the colonial period, until after World War II. Although in some territories several competing political parties developed just prior to independence, more typically one mass party developed, focusing its objectives on gaining independence. While the colonial authorities usually attempted to insure that a multiple party system would operate after independence, most African nations have continued to operate politically with one large party, which grew out of the pre-independence nationalist movement.

Most colonial territories had no constitution, but just before independence constitutions were drawn up to serve as guides for future political and governmental functions. Normally these constitutions were compromises between the demands of various African interests and those of the out-going colonial authorities. Since independence few African nations have regarded their constitutions as hallowed documents; they have often been modified, or even suspended, on the grounds that they failed to reflect the realities of African needs and desires in governance.

As a preamble to the study of African nation building, a teacher might wish to lead the class through a brief review (for one or two class sessions) of the political and governmental systems that existed at the time of independence in two or three selected countries. Such a review can follow the pattern used in studying the governments and politics of the United States or European countries, concentrating on the following areas:

☐ What were the chief tenets of the constitution? How did it provide for individual rights, the right of political dissent, and orderly change of government through elections?

☐ What was the nature of the chief executive? What were his powers? Was he subject to checks and balances by the legislature and the judiciary? To what extent did the constitutional definition of the chief executive fit the personality and political position of the man who had led the achievement of independence?

☐ What was the legislative institution? How did its powers compare with those of the chief executive? Was it dominated by one party? Did it reflect, either within one party or through competing parties, a variety of conflicting interests?

☐ What was the judiciary? How much power did it have compared with the chief executive and the legislature? Was the system of law derived from that of the colonial power or did it reflect African legal thought?

☐ In the political process, what were the chief appeals of the main nationalist party? Was its leader charismatic?

Were there opposition parties or identifiable factions within the main movement? Did the party have a detailed program for nation building? Were ethnic and sectional diversities represented through competing parties or within the major nationalist movement?

☐ What was the structure of civil administration and local government? To what extent were chiefs or local traditional councils involved in the official structure of local government? What offices were appointive and what were nonpolitical (civil service)?

Post-Independence Changes

Almost every former colonial territory in Africa has undergone significant changes in government and politics since the formal attainment of independence. Constitutions have been amended. The office of chief executive has been strengthened, often while the role of the legislature has been diminished. Frequently the administration has become more politicized, with higher level civil servants being appointed only if they are loyal members of the governing political party. In some countries the legal system has been changed, at least in part, to introduce more African traditional law or to reflect the new conditions of national life since independence.

Several areas of typical change can be singled out to provide the class with a framework for studying the African nations chosen for concentration.

ROLE OF THE HEAD OF STATE

With few exceptions, the elected leaders of African nations have increased their powers over those provided at the time of independence. In a few cases, such as with the late

Kwame Nkrumah of Ghana, constitutional changes were introduced to make the incumbents permanent; Nkrumah was proclaimed "President for Life." Where elected civilian governments have been deposed by the military (which has occurred in roughly twenty African nations), the head of the military insurgents has held virtually dictatorial power, at least temporarily. What changes in the role of the head of state have occurred in the countries the class is studying?

African political and intellectual leaders have justified the expanding power of the chief executive on several grounds.

First, it is maintained that African societies are not comfortable with the parliamentary system of government. It is asserted that Africans expected their rulers to be strong and authoritative; such rulers are expected to rule wisely, using various mechanisms for seeking advice and ascertaining the desires of the people, but should be forcibly removed if experience shows that their rule is not wise. Under this concept of leadership, it is argued that periodic elections and assent by parliament are arbitrary and artificial. Many African intellectuals and political leaders dispute these arguments and appeal for adherence to formal systems of election, balances of power, and presidential accountability, but they are, in many African nations, in the minority.

Second, it is argued that the paucity of money and resources demands that the chief executive have enough power to allocate them rationally and impartially, without dispute from special interests in parliament. Since the highest priority for the average African is rapid improvement in the standard of living, it is asserted that the head of state must be able to use whatever national moneys and resources he can command to undertake planned national development without constant argument and challenge.

Third, advocates of strong chief executive powers maintain that national unity is most effectively developed if there is a powerful chief executive who can serve as a personal symbol of the nation. Peoples of diverse ethnic origins must be able to identify with a powerful leader whose authority is supreme and whose position transcends that of any ethnic or sectional interest.

With the American tradition of limited executive power, with carefully structured checks and balances, the tendency toward authoritarian rule in Africa seems contradictory to democratic values. Yet American students must recognize that African values may be different. Historically African nations have developed a different concept of national leadership, in which the strong, semi-divine leader is considered the soul of the nation. Rulers who abused this power were, in the past, removed by forceful means; but they were expected to rule with great power, nevertheless. In modern Africa the same concept seems to be widely held.

ONE-PARTY SYSTEM

Although the departing colonial authorities generally tried to insure that African countries would have two or more opposition political parties based on American and European models, many African nations quickly moved toward the one-party system; some have even passed laws making opposition parties illegal. A number of African leaders who have shown great qualities of humanitarianism and respect for their people have spoken and written defending the validity of the one-party system for Africa.

As with strong executive powers, advocates of the one-party system maintain that African tradition has never regarded formal opposition as necessary for good government.

They argue that two parties cost precious money, that they force potential leaders to expend time and energy on political maneuvering rather than on national development, that they tend to divide the people at a time when everyone must be united in the nation-building effort, and that they are artificial European structures that were imposed on Africa.

It is strongly recommended that students read and discuss one of the more eloquent African arguments in favor of the one-party system, such as that of Julius Nyerere of Tanzania. Since a tendency toward the one-party system is present in almost all African nations, it is important to understand the reasons Africans give for its justification.

AFRICAN SOCIALISM

Virtually every African nation has proclaimed some version of socialism as its national policy since independence; this is true even in those nations that welcome foreign private capital. African definitions of socialism vary, and most are not borrowed directly from Karl Marx or other European ideologists. They always include the concept of state control of certain sectors of the economy, and they usually argue that African tradition demands governmental limitation on the private accumulation of wealth and economic power. All African definitions of African socialism rest upon the belief that capitalism is incapable of guaranteeing the rapid development of society and economy that will provide new goods, services, and amenities to all the people.

MILITARY COUPS

Twenty African nations have experienced sudden changes in government when army officers, backed by their troops, seized the reins of government and deposed the elected head of state. This has occurred so often and in such a large number of countries that the outside world has come to think of a military coup as a normal occurrence in Africa.

Where the military has seized power, it has dissolved the legislature as well as dismissed the chief executive and his cabinet; in a few cases it has also suspended the judicial structure as well. In a few countries the military leaders have eventually returned the reins of power to elected governments after an interim of several years, but in others the military leaders have contined to rule.

The reasons given for military coups have generally been the same: the inability of the elected government to ease the rising cost of living, widespread unemployment and other economic woes, corruption and accumulation of wealth by the top elected leaders, and arbitrary use of power by the elected government to benefit favored individuals, tribes, sections of the country, or economic interests.

Implicit in the military coup is, of course, the recognition (or the fear) that an elected government that has become ineffective or unpopular cannot be changed except by military action. This is an inevitable consequence of the trend toward strong chief executives who become entrenched in power and weakened legislatures, which are expected to rubber stamp the decisions of the chief executive and his cabinet.

Since the military coup has become so common in Africa, students should look carefully at how they occur and the factors that have brought them about. While no one argues that the military coup is a desirable way of changing governments, or that rule by military leaders who have seized power by force is a desirable form of government, there are several supporting points that are often made.

First, African governments throughout history were often changed by force rather than by peaceful election. It may be that African cultures still have this as a deeply ingrained political process.

Second, most military coups in Africa have been either bloodless or have involved very few deaths. The ordinary people of the nation seem to be little affected when their government is changed abruptly.

Third, these dramatic changes in government have rarely resulted in civil disturbances or disruption of normal governmental services and daily life: the mails continue to be delivered, telephones work, garbage is collected, water and power continue to flow, salaries are paid, taxes are levied, and transportation moves. Although there have been broader effects, both positive and negative, on such vital matters as foreign investment, it is generally true that national and economic development continues in most African nations even after coups and under military rule.

Fourth, there is a gap between the urgent expectations of African peoples for material progress and the ability of national governments to provide sufficiently rapid progress, and this gap is likely to lead to abrupt changes in governments for the indefinite future. Some scholars believe that there will be instability at the higher levels of government for many years to come. The important question, these scholars suggest, is the extent to which this inevitable instability will affect the daily lives of ordinary Africans and the overall pace of economic development.

TRIBALISM

In some African nations, although there are several notable

exceptions (e.g., Tanzania, Botswana, Mali, Guinea), there is evidence that ethnic tensions have had an effect on national political life since independence. As was noted previously, foreigners tend to attribute many of the troubles of modern Africa to this. It is undeniable that several nations have experienced difficulties that arose very largely from ethnic tensions (Burundi is a tragic case in point), but it is easy to overestimate the importance of inter-tribal rivalries and conflicts.

As a general rule Africans, like Americans and all other people, hold multiple identities (religious, family, ethnic, national, occupational, social, educational, and sexual). There is no real difference between African ethnic ties and those of most European countries; Belgium and Yugoslavia, to cite but two examples, suffer as much from "tribalism" as most African nations, and the United States is far from free of ethnic tensions. It is rare in modern Africa for difficulties to be caused by ethnic factors (Burundi is an exception). More typically, dissatisfaction with the scarcity of jobs, the paucity of classroom places, the allocation of funds for development projects, and similar grievances may coincide with ethnic divisions, but they may just as easily coincide with other divisions, such as between old and young, urban and rural, or educated and non-educated.

African leaders fear tribalism, but they fear it because they know that it provides a ready-made rubric under which dissatisfied people may come together and decide that they are being discriminated against because of their ethnic origin. Yet African leaders also fear other divisions that may provide the same sense of unity and grievance. In Tanzania, which has no "tribal" problem, the national leadership is deeply concerned over the possibility that rural citizens will feel that they are being discriminated against if the urban areas continue to develop more rapidly than the rural.

ECONOMIC DEVELOPMENT

The Colonial Legacy

Today, even after years of independence for the nations of Africa, there is still controversy over the extent to which the colonial authorities laid the foundations for sound economic development. Apologists for colonial rule claim that great strides were made in building railroads, ports, roads, and airports, in locating and exploiting mineral resources, in agricultural development, in the development of urban commercial and communication facilities, and in the creation of national systems of commerce. Critics argue that the colonialists did only the minimum necessary to earn a profit and to pay the costs of colonial governments; independent African nations, in this view, have had to begin virtually at the beginning in most areas of economic development.

Whatever the reality (and undoubtedly it lies somewhere between these two extremes), it is true that every African nation began its independence at a very low point of economic development, and many have made less than satisfactory progress since. Per capita incomes are frequently under one hundred dollars per year. Between seventy percent and ninety percent of the population in most countries lives on the land, devoting their energies primarily to growing food for survival, with little time or opportunity to earn more than a few dollars a year in cash. National budgets are small and chronically overburdened by the pressing demands of essential services, appeals for development assistance throughout the country, and payments on loans obtained from foreign sources. The gap between urban and rural development continues to widen, since most opportunities for jobs exist in or near the cities.

The colonial legacy in the economic sphere can most easily be assessed by considering several key sectors.

TRANSPORTATION AND COMMUNICATIONS

Most African countries have a thin network of railroads and all-weather roads that were developed early in the colonial era. The greatest period of railway development took place between 1885 and 1910 when lines were laid from the sea to known centers of agricultural produce or minerals in the interior. The most important cities are generally connected by railroads or highways, or both. But most parts of Africa are isolated from these routes, served by no roads or by narrow roads that are impassable during the rainy seasons.

Those African nations located on the coasts have generally had at least one seaport that can handle freighters, but all have had to expand their original port facilities in order to handle heavier items, export minerals, and keep up with an increasing import–export volume.

Air transportation was poorly developed at the time of independence in most African countries, but at least all large cities within each colonial area were connected by airlines as well as with the major cities of Europe. A skeletal network of internal air services had been established and is useful in moving both passengers and goods within a country. Cities in different colonial territories were also rarely linked by roads or air services; frequently it was easier to fly from Africa to Europe, then back to Africa, than to fly 500 miles between two African cities.

A minimal communication system was also established in every African country during the colonial period. Post offices, telegraphs, and telephones connected the capitals with Europe, and there was limited inter-linking of the major centers within each country. The emphasis in communication was on linking the African capital and the capital of the colonial power, so that there were telephone services between Abidjan and Paris, for example, and between Accra and London, but not between Abidjan and Accra, located less than 390 miles from each other.

AGRICULTURAL DEVELOPMENT

Africa had two critical problems in agriculture as its new nations attained independence: most people were dependent upon non-cash crops, and only one or a very few cash crops had been developed for export. In Tanzania, for example, more than eighty-five percent of the people grew little that could be sold, and the country was heavily dependent on sales of sisal—most of which was grown by foreign farmers—for income.

The thrust of colonial economic policy in the agricultural area was to encourage the production of certain crops that required little investment, that Africans could grow without special training, and for which there were ready markets abroad. Thus groundnuts (peanuts) became the major crop in Mali, Senegal, northern Nigeria, and other countries; cocoa in Ghana and southern Nigeria; coffee in Kenya and northern Tanzania; cotton in Egypt, the Sudan, and other countries; sugarcane in Swaziland; and tea in Malawi. In areas of Africa that were not immediately suitable for such cash crops, there was no development. As a result the majority of the people in these areas were excluded from agricultural progress, and the African governments were heavily dependent on the few cash crops that had been introduced.

The recommended study of Africa's geography will have shown students that large parts of Africa are not fertile or lack suitable rainfall. These environmental conditions which affect so much of the continent mean that most Africans are able to grow only enough food to feed themselves and their families. They are generally unable to switch to profitable cash crops, even if they wish to do so, without substantial investments in soil reclamation and fertilization, wells, dams, and irrigation facilities, and the development of hybrid plants that will thrive under African conditions and produce high yields. As a general rule, the colonial powers did little in these expensive areas until the last few years before independence; most of the job of country-wide agricultural development faced the new governments after independence.

MINERAL AND NATURAL PRODUCT DEVELOPMENT

Africa is a continent rich in minerals, and important mineral production began in some countries under colonial rule. Copper came from Zambia and Zaire; diamonds from Zaire, Ghana, and Sierra Leone; gold from Ghana and Sierra Leone; tin from Nigeria; manganese from Ghana; cobalt and uranium from Zaire; and chrome and coal from Rhodesia.

Yet the geology of most parts of Africa was not thoroughly studied during the colonial period. It was not until the late 1950s and the 1960s that a major expansion of new mineral development occurred: iron in Sierra Leone; oil in Algeria, Libya, and Nigeria; bauxite in Ghana and Guinea; and copper and zinc in Botswana.

The forest and fish resources of Africa have long been

useful for domestic purposes, including trade within Africa, but were little developed during the colonial period for commercial purposes. A few countries have important forest resources that earned income before independence: lumber in Ghana; rubber in Zaire (and in Liberia, not under colonial rule); copra in Dahomey, Togo, and other countries; and oil from the oil palm in Nigeria. In general, however, exports of either forest or fish products were unimportant in most of Africa until after independence.

MANUFACTURING

Since a major objective of the colonial conquest of Africa was to secure new markets for European manufactures, industry was the least developed sector of the African economy prior to independence. Manufacturing was limited to a few consumer products for which there was a ready market and guaranteed profits: beer, cigarettes, bread, inexpensive shoes, and simple wood furniture, for example. Most clothes, textiles, hardware, tools, automobiles, radios, bicycles, and more complicated manufactured products were imported from Europe, Asia, or America.

BANKING, MONEY, AND CAPITAL

To a large extent the financial systems of Africa were closely linked with those of Europe prior to independence. Money was part of the currency systems of Britain, France, or Belgium. Banks were almost universally foreign-owned and controlled. There was little domestic capital formation and few provisions for loans except for small needs. Virtually all capital for industry, mines, agricultural development, and transportation had to be raised in Europe or America. The cash reserves of those few African nations that had, under colonialism, managed to build up national reserves (such as Ghana and Zambia) were held in trust in Britain, France, or Belgium. With the exception of these small reserves (Ghana, one of the wealthier countries, had less than $300,000,000), every African nation was faced, upon independence, with near-total dependence upon foreign capital resources for any funds it needed to undertake national development projects.

Although this is an area of study that may be difficult for high school students, it is important for them to gain at least a rudimentary understanding of the massive dependence of African financial and commercial systems on Europe. Political independence did not guarantee economic independence. Perhaps the greatest single problem that African nations have faced is that of extricating their economies from the tight embrace of Europe's great companies and money markets.

Post-Independence Changes

African nations have followed many different policies and approaches in facing the enormous task of effecting substantial economic development after independence. Although some were better and some lesser developed, they all were underdeveloped compared with the wealthy countries of Europe and North America, and their peoples expected and demanded material progress. The chasm between where they began, in about 1955–1960 and where the people wanted to be within ten or twenty years was wide and deep. It is the efforts to bridge this chasm that constitute the fascinating aspect of the study of African nation building in the economic realm.

Since a survey of the various efforts made by more than

forty independent African nations is too formidable a task, several areas of activity and priority and questions the teacher may use with the class in examining the selected countries chosen for study, are listed below.

☐ To what extent has the country produced a clear plan for economic development that contains definite priorities and achievable goals? Did the development program adopted at the time of independence prove workable, or has it undergone significant modification?

☐ What has been the balance of priorities in development, between agricultural, mining, industrial, and infrastructure development? (Infrastructure includes roads, railroads, ports, communications, research institutions, economic development agencies, and development banks.)

☐ Have there been important discoveries of minerals or other natural resources that have been practicable for exploitation and that have given a boost to national income?

☐ What foreign policy approaches have been taken in the economic area? Has the country seriously sought capital funds, grants, loans, and trade agreements abroad? Have these been with the former colonial power, with other Western countries, with the Soviet Union and its allies, or elsewhere? To what extent has the country emphasized self-reliance as opposed to reliance on foreign assistance?

☐ What trends have been evident in the annual balances of imports and exports? In cash reserves? In the balance of payments? In per capita income?

☐ How has the policy of African socialism been applied? Has the government encouraged private investment from foreign capital sources? From Africans? Has it tended to restrict private investment to special areas of the economy and reserve other areas for government development?

☐ What priority has been placed on rural development as opposed to urban development? Have industries been dispersed to various parts of the country? Have efforts been made to introduce cash crops among a large proportion of the rural population? Have rural development programs been primarily economic in nature or have they included social development (village housing, schools, medical stations, recreation facilities, adult education, or new forms of social organization)?

☐ In the years since independence, what changes have occurred in the attitudes and policies of national leadership on the broad front of economic development? Have foreign policies changed as a consequence of successes or failures in economic development efforts?

☐ To what extent has the country shown interest in expanding its economic and communication ties with other African states? Has it joined regional economic or trade groupings? Has it participated in projects that build roads or other transportation ties among neighboring countries?

☐ It has often been said that the world's rich or "have" nations are becoming richer, while the poor or "have not" nations are becoming poorer. Is there evidence that the gap between selected African countries and the rich nations of the world is widening?

☐ Taking the past ten years as a guide, and assessing the environmental resources and problems of the selected African nations, how would the class evaluate their progress? What events in economic development would it predict over the next decade? What are the areas of greatest need and promise? Has the leadership done as well as might be expected in economic development or have its policies been inadequate?

5 Nation building in Africa II: national, social, and cultural development

The task of transforming African states into nations includes massive changes in the lives of individuals, the societies and institutions in which they live, and the cultures that give their lives meaning. Building new economic and political systems is critically important, but no more so than building new social systems.

The shaping of new, nationwide social systems, and through them the behavior and attitudes of people, is by no means a wholly planned and consciously directed effort. Africans have been changing for countless centuries and are changing more rapidly now than ever before. To a large extent national leaders are hard pressed just to keep up with these changes, much less plan and direct them. Just as African political and economic systems are vastly different today compared with a few decades ago, the peoples of Africa are very different from those of a generation or two ago. The most effective political leaders are those who can most capably understand what the new African is like and offer programs of national development that are in accord with his aspirations, tastes, attitudes, and abilities.

This chapter logically pairs with the preceding one, except that it deals with people, social organizations, and culture rather than with government, commerce, and economic forces. Insofar as possible it avoids formal sociological analysis and concentrates on forces and trends that affect the quality of individual and family life. Only through gaining some understanding of what is happening to the individual and the family can a student appreciate the dynamic process of change through which the new African states are building themselves into nations.

Two teaching suggestions are strongly recommended.

First, the class should concentrate on a few nations, preferably the same as those chosen for the study of economic and political development.

Second, students should be urged to approach the study of social and cultural developments by focusing on individuals rather than on large groups and concepts. There are many excellent materials available that provide this focus. In the materials section following this chapter the teacher will find listed several works of fiction and autobiographies by African authors. During the past few decades hundreds of African writers have published novels of high quality that portray the changing conditions of modern African social life, especially as they affect individuals and families. Many of these novels are realistic, taking their content from actual events and situations in contemporary Africa, so that they give an accurate description of social life and culture. And many are of considerable literary merit and are interesting, absorbing reading.

A number of great African political and intellectual leaders have also written books that are wholly or partially autobiographical, providing fascinating accounts of growing up and obtaining formal education in twentieth-century Africa as experienced by men who have achieved positions of prominence.

Through African novels and nonfiction works a student

can come to understand much of the change that has been sweeping Africa for the past few decades as Africans themselves have experienced and been affected by it. While a certain amount of reading from other types of writing will be necessary, students will both enjoy and profit from concentrating on the works by Africans that are recommended in the materials section.

Traditional Bases of African Society and Culture

Just as no two individuals can be identical, no two societies can be exactly alike. Understanding African societies and cultures, considering the frequently quoted fact that the continent contains over eight hundred different ethnic groups, can therefore be a formidable task. Each of these ethnic groups speaks its own language and has its own special patterns of social organization, customs, life-styles, religious beliefs, marriage customs, and patterns of individual growth and behavior. Because of this diversity, one cannot study the society and culture of Ghana and thereby achieve a complete understanding of all Africa. To complicate matters, Ghana itself, like most African countries, is divided into numerous societies; one cannot study the people of Accra and thereby understand the people of Kumasi.

Yet the task is not so difficult as might be supposed. Africa's more than eight hundred ethnic groups are not quite as heterogeneous as some writers have asserted. The great majority share similar ideas about God, about the values of life, about the nature of the world, about making a living, and about art and behavior. Even though each

African ethnic group may have slightly different religious beliefs, the fact is that almost all believe in one God and in a host of spirits of nature and of deceased ancestors through whom living men worship God. Knowing these broad similarities helps students gain a surprisingly comprehensive idea of how most Africans live and believe.

These broad similarities in African society and culture are ancient in origin. More modern influences on Africa, especially those of the colonial period, have added new areas of similar experience that produce enough homogeneity among the new nations to make it possible to study a few and thereby gain at least a minimal understanding of all.

The next few pages are devoted to listing and describing briefly a few of the more important similarities in African social structures and cultures as they existed in the past. In studying these traditional bases of African society and culture, the teacher should understand that they represent generalizations that are necessarily arbitrary. Not *every* African society can be so characterized nor were these generalizations true at exactly the same time for every African society for which they are valid. Change has been at work in every African society for millenia, and the rates of change have varied. The dramatic changes set into motion by European contact, for example, affected some African societies as early as the sixteenth century, others during the seventeenth and eighteenth centuries, and still others only in the past fifty years. The traditional bases of African society and culture listed below thus represent a deliberate blurring of time in order to present an approximate representation of what most of Africa was like a century or so ago before the radical changes of the twentieth century accelerated the changes that were already at work.

THE TRIBE AND THE LINEAGE

It has previously been noted that the term "tribe" is not a useful one for describing traditional African societies. African societies, or ethnic groups, have traditionally ranged from tiny bands of a few dozen people, largely nomadic in their way of life, to great states and empires of millions of people who were permanently settled on farms and in towns. The term "tribe" usually means a society that speaks the same language, is ruled by a common government (usually a chief), inhabits a common territory, is bound together by a common culture, and regards itself as being different from all other peoples. But in many African societies this definition applies more properly to the extended family, or lineage, than to larger ethnic groups. While a lineage readily recognizes that other lineages speak the same language and practice a similar way of life, it regards them as different because they acknowledge descent from a different ancestor.

The average African has traditionally identified himself strongly with his descent group: parents, grandparents, children, cousins, aunts, and uncles. If the descent group was matrilineal (tracing its descent through the female line), a child regarded his father as an appendage to the group, no matter how strong the ties of affection to him as an individual. In such a case, the mother's father and her brothers were regarded as important as the father in giving advice and assistance in matters of making a living, marrying, child-rearing, disputes, and other fundamental life events. Some African groups were matrilineal, others patrilineal, and a few traced descent (as we do) through both parents. Whatever the case, the solidarity of the lineage was one of the most important foundations of an individual's life.

The solidarity of the lineage was an idea that persisted century after century, even while Africans were migrating to new territories, merging together into various states and kingdoms, and coming into contact with very different peoples. The lineage provided protection, comfort, security in times of adversity, and companionship; in return it required an individual to behave according to the standards established by the ancestors, to act loyally in family matters, and to obey the rulings and directives of the head of the family. In cases where the welfare of the lineage conflicted with obligations to the state, the individual generally acted on behalf of the lineage, unless the king were strong enough to force him to do otherwise. A wise king tended to work through family authority rather than to challenge it.

Even though the lineage was traditionally the basic institution of African life, it was not generally the largest political unit. Most Africans belonged to states that were composed of a number of lineages, and some states and empires encompassed lineages that were completely different from each other in language and culture. Very rarely did the ruler of a state attempt to weaken the solidarity of the lineages within his territory; he normally accepted their rules of inheritance, their marriage customs, and their religious and philosophical views. His concerns tended to be that his subjects pay taxes or tribute, that they acknowledge his ultimate sovereignty, that they serve when needed in military or public works enterprises, and that they renounce loyalty to other states.

Because of this system in which a state could exist without disturbing the fundamental solidarity of the lineage, Africans have a long history of being members of large political units while still regarding their families as their most important social structure.

Students should spend enough time on this important point to understand it, because it has great relevance to the modern process of nation building. The teacher might wish to spend at least one class period examining with the students the areas of life in which the lineage was predominant and those in which the state took precedence, the ways in which lineages expected individuals to behave, the obligations of the individual toward his kinsmen within the lineage, and how Africans tended to behave toward members of different lineages.

VALUES OF FAMILY LIFE

The traditional solidarity of the extended family structure was a comprehensive system that gave direction to many areas of African life. In these areas, several of the more important of which are outlined below, cultural values of great strength were formed; many of these values are still very influential in contemporary African social and cultural development.

Marriage as a Contract between Families. In this area, the partners in a marriage were viewed as links between\two families, and the marriage agreement was regarded as a contract between the two families. Most societies required the husband (aided by his family) to deposit valuable goods with the family of the wife to indicate his intent to be a good husband and to insure that his family accepted responsibility for him. Although usually referred to as a "bride price," this system was not a purchase of a bride. In case of divorce, the valuables reverted to the husband if the wife were at fault or were retained by her family if the husband were at fault.

Diffusion of Bonds of Affection. Although Africans experience the same kind of love between spouses or between parents and children that Americans do, the form of marriage, the existence of polygamy, and the prevalence of the extended family tended to emphasize affectionate relationships among a larger group and to reduce the tendency toward deep, intimate bonds that exist within the small nuclear family.

The African child tended to love, and to be loved by, a large group of relatives in addition to his natural father and mother. He could have bonds of affection with cousins that were as strong as those with siblings, and with aunts and uncles as strong as those with his natural parents.

Freedom and Security. The closeness of lineage ties gave the individual his greatest sense of security, and he felt alone and unprotected if he became at odds with the family. He was able to exercise a measure of individual freedom so long as he abided by family obligations but was subject to restrictive pressures if he violated family custom. There was, in traditional Africa, little opportunity for an individual who chafed under its supervision to escape the embrace of the extended family, because an individual unprotected by family ties had no assurance of good treatment from peoples to whom he was not related.

Sharing of Wealth. While few African societies were truly communal (all sharing wealth equally), individuals who had suffered misfortune were provided with food and shelter by relatives. The lineage served as an important welfare system.

Regulation of Morality. The behavior of the individual was very much prescribed by the customs of his lineage; disloyalty and uncharitable acts within the extended family were considered immoral behavior. Much of Africa's traditional law derives from family custom: property rights, inheritance, debts, assault, marital behavior, and land usage, for example

Respect for the Aged and Ancestors. Elderly people were usually respected and accorded many rights and privileges; they were considered wise and were regarded as guardians of the family's integrity. Ancestors, especially those who had distinguished themselves when alive, were regarded with veneration and were integral parts of the African religious belief. A great ancestor was believed to live in a spiritual realm, in contact with God and responsible to God for supervising the affairs of his descendants. He was thought to be able to protect virtuous descendants from misfortune and to invoke misfortune on the wayward. Most African religions included rituals for praying to and sacrificing to the ancestors.

PERVASIVENESS OF RELIGION

Despite Western characterization of Africans as "heathens," "pagans," and "animists," religion is a deep, pervasive influence in traditional African life. It is intimately interconnected with family values through the belief in the spiritual role of ancestors and is expressed through art, drama, music, and dance as well as through regular religious rituals and prayers.

Most Africans believe in one God, who created the universe and man but who is somewhat remote from the daily lives of men and from the acts of nature. Because God is believed to have more important concerns, he is said to have created spirits of nature, as well as those of ancestors, to govern the fortunes of men and the forces of nature. Man lives according to God's desires when he respects the ancestors and family customs, is moral and pious in his behavior, and propitiates the spirits of nature by good conduct and sacrifices.

There are four chief aspects of religion that students should understand:

1. It is intimately bound up with almost all of African traditional life, so that the individual African has long felt a deep need for religious belief and practice.

2. Because the traditional religious system is nonscientific, it attributes to spiritual causes natural events, illnesses, injuries, misfortune, good fortune, and other matters that Western belief tends to consider caused by accident or physical forces.

3. It involves deep respect for the aged and ancestors.

4. It has inspired much of Africa's artistic achievement, and Africa has in turn inspired or influenced many aspects of world art. African art, for example, has influenced Picasso, Modigliani, and other great Western artists; African folktales and fables (especially from Aesop and the Brer Rabbit traditions) have become part of Western culture; American jazz and other music reflect African influence; many modern dances in the Americas stem from African dance styles.

SOCIAL CLASSES

Traditional Africa was far from being a classless society, except in the smallest, least developed groups. The majority of African states had well defined social classes and even castes: royal lines, a noble class, military class, merchants and traders, artisan classes (iron workers, potters, glass workers, leather workers, sculptors), peasant farmers, and slaves or serfs.

The African societies that had these recognized classes had an elaborate structure of mutual rights and obligations for each; even slaves had well defined rights and could rise to positions of great power and wealth if they had ability. While higher classes had a clearly superior position than that of lower classes, severe exploitation was rare. African freemen, most of whom were peasant farmers, generally had a sturdy sense of their rights and tended to resist relegation to an oppressive position.

The frequent migrations of African families in search of less crowded land plus the numerous networks of commerce provided opportunities for Africans to move from one class to another. Only in restricted geographical zones such as Egypt's Nile Valley did permanent castes of poor peasants develop. Slaves could attain freedom under certain circumstances in most of Africa.

Social Change in the New Africa

The African-European trade system, which began in the late fifteenth century, set into motion a new pattern of change that was grounded in the opportunities for increased wealth and in the gradually growing evidence of European material and technological superiority. Until the twentieth century, however, this pattern of change was largely confined to the coastal areas and up a few major riverways into the interior. With the colonial conquest, this change accelerated rapidly and penetrated virtually every part of the African continent.

The colonial period introduced a new economic system and a new structure of government, and these in turn set into motion fundamental changes in African social organization, the position of the individual, and African cultural practices and values. By the time African states achieved independence, their peoples were caught up in a process of change that has often been referred to as revolutionary; it amounts to a degree of change that affects nearly every aspect of the lives of most Africans.

As has been noted, African governments and leaders are hard pressed to stay abreast of this change; most have tried to exercise some control and leadership over it, but only a few governments have been successful enough to stay in power for long.

The modernizing changes that are so powerfully at work in Africa are best considered by focusing on five areas: economic forces and the cash economy; the changing role of the individual and the family; the influence of European institutions, especially the churches and the schools; the growth of large urban areas; and the pressure for modernization in the rural areas. If a student keeps the foregoing outline of traditional characteristics in mind as he looks at contemporary Africa, he can profitably use it as a base point against which to gauge the degree of change that has occurred in recent years and that may be expected over the next few years.

ECONOMIC FORCES AND THE CASH ECONOMY

In the traditional Africa of long ago, goods were exchanged by bartering, except in the large markets. There, various forms of cash were used, but these were handled primarily by professional traders and the nobility. During the colonial period, however, the use of cash currency became general, so that even the most isolated rural peasants sold small quantities of goods for cash, which they used to buy other goods. The effect of the cash economy has been drastic.

The primary objective of the colonial conquest was to open up African territories to European exploitation. European industry needed raw materials (cocoa, rubber, palm oil, copra, cotton, kapok, grain, hides, metals, precious stones, and other products) as well as expanding markets in which to sell European manufactured goods (pots, pans, shoes, iron tools, cloth, alcoholic beverages, tobacco, and later, bicycles, radios, and automobiles). With varying degrees of aggressiveness, each colonial power used its control of African territory to promote the production of more raw materials and the consumption of more European products. Africans were required to sell their products and labor for cash, which was then used to buy the European goods.

Colonial governments were invariably financed from African revenues, usually from duties on the import and export of goods and from taxes on individuals and households. The introduction of taxation made it necessary for every adult African male to acquire at least a small amount of cash each year to pay his taxes, even if he were not interested in purchasing European goods. Virtually all Africans quickly acquired a taste for European goods, however, so that the attraction of being able to buy them, combined with the need for cash for taxes, rapidly pulled almost everyone into the cash economy to one degree or another.

CHANGES IN THE FAMILY AND ROLE OF THE INDIVIDUAL

The establishment of colonial governments weakened the authority of African rulers, and this initially served to strengthen the role of the extended family. Soon, however, the spread of European laws and the cash economy began to weaken the authority of family heads and the solidarity of family ties.

Both European governmental-legal systems and the cash economy tended to emphasize the individual. It was the individual who was held accountable for abiding by the new systems of law, and it was the individual who was punished if his taxes were not paid. Jobs were available to individuals, not families. Cash crops were sold by individuals, who acquired some measure of control over decisions about how the cash would be used. The concepts of individual accountability for lawful behavior and taxes and the opening up of a variety of new opportunities to individuals were new to most Africans and directly conflicted with the traditional concepts of family responsibility and collective behavior.

The emphasis on the individual offered an alternative to family control that had previously been rare. An individual could move to a town or a mining area to find employment, without regard to whether his family seniors approved. In the towns marriages could be arranged between two individuals rather than between two extended families. Children were reared without the aid or influence of the large extended kin group. In many respects the individual could act solely on his own responsibility, reaping for himself whatever good or bad fortunes resulted.

As will be noted in more detail below, the weakening of family ties has been more pronounced in the towns and among educated people than in the rural areas and among those who have had no schooling. Yet expansion of the freedom of the individual and weakening of the deep solidarity of traditional African family life have spread throughout the continent. The degree to which these processes have occurred is an important topic for students to consider in the countries being studied.

In the references recommended in the materials section, the students will find that most African writers of both fiction and nonfiction deal with the changing role of the individual and the family. They will discover that many Africans see both value and danger in the changes that are underway. One of the most discussed topics in modern Africa is how, in the process of nation building, Africa's new societies can strengthen the freedoms of the individual without losing the cherished solidarity of the traditional family structure; few Africans wish their family system to become like that in the Western world.

INFLUENCE OF EUROPEAN INSTITUTIONS

African religions have been weakened by the same forces that have affected the individual and the family, as well as by European ideas of science and technology. At the same time, both Christian and Islamic missionaries have sought converts and both religions have grown rapidly at the expense of African traditional faith, filling the void in the African soul as his own religion's foundations were shattered.

Christianity has had a strong appeal to Africans because it was associated with the great power of Europeans. Many Africans have felt that becoming a Christian would help them achieve the affluence and high status of Europeans. Even today, when Africans feel a hostility toward the colonial conquest and European attitudes of superiority, they still adhere to Christianity, which has sunk deep roots in African religious life.

Islam required less change on the part of African believers, since it preaches tolerance of differences, permits polygamy, and is in various ways consistent with African values. African Muslims outnumber African Christians, and though both religions are continuing to expand their memberships, Islam is growing more rapidly than Christianity.

Christianity has been adopted among the more westernized Africans, who today have adapted it to Africa's new social and cultural conditions. Almost all African Christian churches are independent of European control, and many have introduced African touches of dance, music, and ceremony to the rituals.

Both religions have been influential in inducing change, though Christianity has produced sharper changes than Islam. Both have enhanced the concept of individual responsibility and freedom, both have tended to put Africans into communication with non-Africans, and both have added new conditions to marriage, relations between parent and child, and between the individual and the state.

Western education has been, if anything, even more influential than Christianity in promoting change in Africa. Like Christianity, it has been associated with European power and affluence; most Africans have felt that it was the main source of European superiority at the time of the colonial conquest. In addition, Africans with education have had the advantage in securing jobs of higher prestige and pay: teaching, church work, agents for commercial firms, government jobs, and professional positions.

The nationalist political leadership that led African states to independence and still dominates African affairs has come almost entirely from the ranks of the educated. The average African regards education with almost reverent respect and demands that it be available to all as rapidly as possible.

In the nation-building process African governments have had to give top priority to the expansion of education, often devoting as much as thirty-five percent of their national budgets to the task. Some states, such as Ghana, have achieved nearly universal primary schooling as a result, and all are continuing to build new schools and train more teachers.

The post-independence period has shown, however, that formal education alone does not guarantee either the rapid building of the nation or a prestigious job for the educated person. Increasing numbers of young people who have completed from six to twelve years of schooling find it impossible to find a job, since educational expansion has proceeded faster than economic expansion. Every African government is now engaged in considerable study and experimentation in the hope of finding ways to provide a more useful kind of education that will contribute to nation building and promote a better life for the educated.

Students will find the theme of seeking education emphasized in many of the novels and biographies recommended in the materials section. It is one of the most powerful forces operating in modern Africa. The child undergoing formal education experiences one new influence after another, year after year, until he emerges with almost every idea and value different from his unschooled peers. While only a minority of Africans are yet able to complete more than three or four years of school, they set the pace for nation building. The teacher is urged to help students focus on the meaning of formal education in changing the life-style and direction of the individual African.

GROWTH OF URBAN AREAS

Africa, like the rest of the world, is in the throes of a rapid process of urbanization. Towns and cities are growing far more rapidly than the population at large, so that each year a larger percentage of the population is found in towns and cities. While towns and cities existed in traditional Africa, the growth of the cash economy and the effects of modernization have produced more and larger cities, which are very much like those in Europe and America. Since World War II urban growth has accelerated. Many African cities (e.g., Accra, Abidjan, Nairobi, Addis Ababa, Salisbury, Lusaka, Lagos) have increased their populations many times, growing from less than 100,000 before the war to as much as 500,000 since.

The urbanization process involves a pull from the cities and a push from the rural areas. In the cities there are thought to be jobs, goods, educational opportunities, excitement, recreation, and abundant social services. In the rural areas the land is poor and overcrowded, jobs are scarce, life is plain and unexciting, other opportunities are few, and people feel isolated from the affairs of the modern world. Many Africans, like individuals in every part of the world, think of the cities as exciting, stimulating places, contrasting sharply with the poor and backward countryside.

As the cash economy and nation building expand to exert ever more influence in the rural areas, the pull of the cities is enhanced and the rate of urban growth continues to accelerate.

African cities are thus experiencing conditions that are common wherever cities have grown rapidly. Overcrowding produces slums and shantytowns, with consequent problems of disease and conditions of poverty. Individual freedom is great, compared with the rural areas, and the authority of the family is weakened. Typical social problems abound: robbery by the poor, assault and violence, prostitution, juvenile delinquency, and stresses within the family. Most authorities agree that these problems of African cities, while severe, have generally not reached the serious levels of similar problems in American cities. One reason is that the role of the family is still stronger in African cities than is the case in the United States, and Africans are seeking ways to prevent further deterioration of family solidarity.

Some traditional social influences are still at work in African cities. Family ties are not completely destroyed: a new migrant from the country tends to live with, and be supported by, his kin in the city until he becomes self-sufficient. Many people join ethnic associations, which function like lodges and mutual aid societies, providing the individual member with companionship, legal advice, loans, help in finding a job, and support in adversity. In these associations all the members come from the same lineage, district, or ethnic group.

Urban life has increased the opportunities for African women, helping to free them from traditional duties and offering them chances to work or engage in commerce. Much of the petty trading is carried on by women, and women have become active in national and local politics.

African cities are experiencing the growth of a new culture that is heavily influenced by the modern cash economy and Western institutions but that blends these with traditional African cultural elements. New styles in popular music and dance, new church rituals, new relationships between men and women and adults and children, and new social classes based on individual achievement are all part of this new culture. The emerging culture of the cities exerts a considerable influence on national thinking, so that even isolated rural areas are affected.

MODERNIZATION AND RURAL AFRICA

It has been fashionable to draw a sharp distinction between urban and rural Africa, even to the extent of characterizing the rural areas as being completely traditional or tribal and outside the cash economy. This is a false dichotomy that can lead to misunderstanding of the entire African nation-building process.

There are clear differences between rural and urban Africa, but the differences are of degree, not kind. As has been noted already, rural Africans are affected by the cash economy, even though they may spend most of their time and labor in subsistence occupations growing food or tending animals for their own family's livelihood. Urban influences affect the thinking of rural people, so that one of the chief problems in African nation building is a feeling on the part of rural peoples that they and their development are neglected in favor of the cities.

At the time of independence most political movements had their headquarters and greatest strength in the urban areas, and most leaders were convinced that nation building had to begin in the cities by attracting industries, building airports and ports, establishing universities, and increasing urban employment. This has led to a neglect of rural development in most African countries, but increasingly the rural citizens are demanding that more of the national budgets be spent in the countryside to improve local roads, agriculture, irrigation, health services, and education.

A fertile area for classroom attention is the relationship between the urban and rural areas in the countries being studied.

☐ To what extent has the government concentrated its development funds and priorities on the urban areas and industries?

☐ What political pressures are exerted on national policy by rural voters?

☐ Has the past decade witnessed any shift in national attention toward rural development? What forms do rural development take?

In focusing on these questions, the teacher is urged to examine, with the class, the national development program of Tanzania, which has emphasized rural development as strongly as any country in Africa. There President Julius Nyerere and the ruling Tanganyika African National Union party made a formal decision, in 1967, to begin a radical new program of nation building that emphasized principles of self-help and the transformation of rural life. The new nation-building effort is based on many traditional African values, such as the solidarity of the extended family and the acceptance of collective responsibility for development.

As a final note, the teacher is urged to help students understand that the changes in modern Africa, and the nation-building process, are affecting all of Africa, despite the fact that rural Africa lags behind the cities. The old Africa of the popular Western stereotype, where tribal peoples lived in small villages completely untouched by out-side forces, has long disappeared—if it ever existed at all. Virtually every African uses money, wears European or other modern types of clothes, is familiar with bicycles, cars, doctors, and other modern things, and is fully aware that he is part of a new nation and a wider world. Literacy is spreading. And the demand for economic and educational development is felt in every part of the continent. One cannot understand modern Africa if he continues to think of the rural African as an exotic person from another era.

Teaching Materials

When making selections from the following recommended materials, the teacher is urged to keep in mind the point made in Chapters Four and Five that Africa today is *not* predominantly the tribal Africa of the popular American stereotype. Modern Africa is highly diverse, and the materials used should help students comprehend this diversity.

Materials available for studying contemporary Africa are

more abundant than those for geography and history, and some are of excellent quality. There are numerous films, magazines, and other items produced by Africans themselves that are invaluable for use in American schools. Those listed below are readily available and are generally inexpensive.

The organization of this section is different from that for geography and history, because the two preceding chapters on contemporary Africa include discussions of economics, politics, art, culture, family life, rural and urban life, and education. The materials recommended are therefore grouped under several categories that reflect these different perspectives: Colonialism and Nationalism, Economic Development, Education and Nation Building, Women in Africa, and African Culture and Art.

Materials for both teacher reference and classroom use are listed under each category. Relatively few teacher references are given, however, since there are a number of excellent books and collections produced for high school classes that can be used for reference by teachers as well as by students. Addresses of film producers are given in the Appendix.

COLONIALISM AND NATIONALISM

Student Materials

Colonial Kenya, Cultures in Conflict. Recommended for in-depth study of Kenyan resistance to British colonial rule and White settler power following World War II. Developed by the Public Issues Series of the Harvard University Social Studies Project. American Educational Press, Educational Center, Columbus, Ohio 43216. 1968. $.30 for orders of ten or more.

Through African Eyes, vol. IV: *The Colonial Experience*: *An Inside View* and vol. V: *The Rise of Nationalism*: *Freedom Regained.* Leon Clark, ed. Makes extensive use of primary African source materials for inquiry study. Recommended teacher guide separate. Praeger Publishers, 111 Fourth Ave., New York, N.Y. 10003. 1969. $2.45.

Teacher References

Specific chapters from history references are also useful on colonial experience and African resistance patterns.

Tarikh: vol. I, no. 2: *African Leadership and European Domination;* vol. 1, no. 4: *Modernizers in Africa;* vol. II, no. 2: *African Achievement and Tragedy;* vol. II, no. 4: *France in Africa;* vol. III, no. 3: *Indirect Rule in British Africa;* and vol. III, no. 4: *Independence Movements in Africa.* An African-produced journal of history published biannually. Recommended for libraries. Representative of new research from African universities. Designed for African secondary schools. Each volume is $2 and contains short essays. Humanities Press, 450 Park Ave. South, New York, N.Y. 10016.

Things Fall Apart. A.C. Achebe. Nigerian novel showing traditional-modern culture stress during late colonial period. This book is the most popular modern African novel and has sold 400,000 copies. Fawcett World Library, 1 Astor Place, New York, N.Y. 10003. 1963. $1.25. pap.

Tradition and Change in Africa. I. Wallerstein and E. Rich. Thematically organized. General text using primary and secondary documents from African sources. May also be used as class text with average to above-average readers. Random House, 201 East 50th St., New York, N.Y. 10022. 1972. $7.95.

Weep Not Child. James Ngugi. Novel by a Kenyan concerning an African youth and his reactions to British settler society and the African resistance movement, the Mau-Mau. Fawcett World Library, 1 Astor Place, New York, N.Y. 10003. 1968. $1.25. pap.

Films

In Chapter Nine is a listing of film libraries and producers, many of which have old films from the 1945–1960 period. These are a history of American images of Africa. Through the use of these dated films and by reference to Hollywood stereotypes of Africans during the colonial period, a class can be exposed to the roles and functions of Africans as perceived during this period.

Mussolini and Ethiopia. 25 min., B&W. Extensive documentary footage originally produced for television. Films Incorporated, $155.

ECONOMIC DEVELOPMENT

Student Materials

Most American students first study about Africans in junior high school. During the African curriculum materials explosion of the past five years, very little of the "new social studies" has reached this segment of American children. Textbooks might have been specifically designed for "slow" readers or they might have colored photo essays, but they remained essentially expository in nature.

Curriculum decision-makers now can turn to several products for a different approach to Africa. Their emphasis is on

inquiry materials, original African writing, and the creation
of fictitious vignettes that convey much of the context and
flavor of youth cultures in contemporary Africa.

Africa. Allen R. Boyd and John Nickerson. One of a series
of paperbacks in the "Scholastic World Cultures Program," which covers various world culture areas. Extensive use is made of interesting fictitious vignettes
about African youth. A filmstrip and record or cassette
are coordinated with the text. A teacher's guide is also
available. Scholastic Book Services, 50 West 44th St.,
New York, N.Y. 10036. Text, $1.35; teacher's guides,
$1.; filmstrip with record, $12.50, with cassette, $14.50;
lab book containing ditto sheets, $7.50; set of three
posters, $2.25.

The Impact of Modernization on Traditional Society. Cross-
cultural approach using Latin American, Asian, and
African examples. Highly recommended for themes
concerned with urbanization. A series of ten 32-page
paperbacks. American Universities Field Staff, 3 Lebanon St., Hanover, N.H. 03755. 1969. $3.50.

Kenya. Larry Cuban and Edward Soja. Part of the Scott,
Foresman Spectra Program, "People of the World." Recommended for educators who decide to take a nation-
state approach to the study of Africa or are seeking
supplementary material. Extensive use of photo essays
and original source material. Scott, Foresman, Glen-
view, Ill. 60005. 1972. $1.47.

Through African Eyes, vol. II: *From Tribe to Town; Problems of Adjustment.* Leon Clark, ed. Student-oriented
text that may also be used by teachers seeking a quick
introduction to the themes of urbanization and cultural
change in Africa. The materials reflect primary African

sources and are designed to be taught by the inquiry approach. Praeger Publishers, 111 Fourth Ave., New York, N.Y. 10003. 1969. $2.45.

The Ways of Man, An Introduction to Many Cultures. Bertha Davis. The publisher calls this its "sixth-grade book," but it should be carefully considered for use in the seventh and eighth grades and might also be useful with some students in the ninth grade. 122 pages are Africa-centered. China, Japan, India, and the Middle East are also covered. Macmillan Company, 866 Third Ave., New York, N.Y. 10017. $7.44.

Teacher References

The African Experience, vol. I. John N. Paden and Edward W. Soga, eds. A series of introductory essays on African societies contributed by scholars from a variety of social science and humanities disciplines. Designed for undergraduate courses in African studies. Northwestern University Press, 1735 Benson Ave., Evanston, Ill. 60201. 1970. $5.50. pap.

Unity or Poverty. R. Green and A. Seidman. The authors describe and evaluate African efforts at national development. Having inherited a nation-state system of sovereignty, new African states are struggling with the need to establish a viable national entity and at the same time confront the need to regionalize their local economies. Penguin African Library, 7110 Ambassador Rd., Baltimore, Md. 21207. 1968. $1.95. pap.

Which Way Africa, rev. ed., Basil Davidson. An analysis of current economic and social trends in Africa with reasoned speculation about future developments. Basil Davidson is a gifted writer and interpreter of African history. This book illustrates his grasp of cultural continuity in African society. Penguin African Library, 7110 Ambassador Rd., Baltimore, Md. 21207. 1969. $1.95. pap.

Films and Filmstrips

For additional recommended films refer to the family study films annotated in Chapter One, African Geography.

Africa Changes; Young Leader, Young Nation, 14 min., color, 1970. Bailey Film Associates. $180, sale; $10, rental. Concerns daily activities of a Tanzanian government official in his efforts to serve his community through implementation of government development programs.

Daily Life of the Bozo, 15 min., color, 1969. International Film Foundation. $175. The Bozo are an African people in the Niger River area of Mali. The film lends itself to an inquiry approach. The Bozo are an agricultural-fishing community. Film can be used from middle elementary grades through senior high school. Sound, but no narration.

Family of Ghana, 30 min., B&W. McGraw-Hill Film Division. $135, sale; $8, rental. A Canadian produced film of the late 1950s, which effectively discusses economic factors affecting the life of a Ghanaian family. The differences in values between son and father remain contained within the essential unity of the family.

Images of Africa, 1973. Four filmstrips with records or cassettes, color: "Traditional Life," "Modern Life," "Historical Africa," and "National Building." International Media. Set with records or cassettes, $69.50; single strips, $20. This set is designed to accompany

the six-volume series "Through African Eyes," published by Praeger, but can be used without these student texts. A printed script, teaching lesson plans
utilizing the inquiry method, and narration with music
are included. These are recommended for preview if
the teacher is using a continental thematic approach to
the study of Africa.

Nuer, two 45 min. reels, color, 1971. McGraw-Hill Film
Division. $680, sale; $75, rental. The Nuer are an African people who rely heavily on cattle for a livelihood.
They live in the southern Sudan and southwest Ethiopia
where this film was taken by anthropologists from an
American university. The film should be extensively pre-
viewed before showing. It is recommended for grades
9–12 interested in cross-cultural study. Traditional ways
of life dominate throughout, although a close examination of the younger generation shows unmistakable evidences of external changes now rapidly affecting this
insular society.

Senegal, 29 min., color, 1966. McGraw-Hill Film Division.
$260, sale; $11, rental. Produced by the International
Labor Organization, this film demonstrates how outside aid can be linked to local initiative to make a difference in economic prosperity in poor, rural areas.

Starting from Scratch, 30 min., color, 1970. Association
Films. Gratis loan. Tanzanian efforts at national development through self-reliance and popular mobilization
are featured. Recommended for use in economics
classes, world culture units, and courses specifically in
African studies. UNESCO-produced for N.E.T.

Tanzania: Self-Reliance, 23 min., color, 1967. McGraw-Hill
Film Division. $260, sale; $12.50, rental. A Dutch film

useful in senior high school to present Tanzanian views on why their country must not rely on foreign aid for its development.

EDUCATION AND NATION BUILDING

Student Material

Through African Eyes, vol. 6: *Nation-Building: Tanzania and the World.* Leon Clark, ed. Emphasis is on primary source materials keyed to inquiry approach. Materials reflect determined Tanzanian approach to national identity and self-reliance. Praeger Publishers, 111 Fourth Ave., New York, N.Y. 10003. 1970. $2.45.

Teacher References

"African Writers" series. Many novels in this series describe experiences of Africans in colonially created school systems. The publisher will send a catalog of its titles for review. Humanities Press, 450 Park Ave. South, New York, N.Y. 10016.

East African Childhood. C. Fox, ed. Three autobiographical accounts. Oxford University Press, 200 Madison Ave., New York, N.Y. 10016. 1967. $1.95. pap.

Maryknoll. Maryknoll Society, Maryknoll, N.Y. 10562. Monthly, $1. For Roman Catholic and secular schools looking for high interest and development-oriented materials, this magazine is highly recommended. It features short (400–600 words) true vignettes about African children and young adults. Excellent color photography supports the narratives. Articles are concerned with people groping with poverty and modernization. Each issue also contains Asian and Latin American materials.

Films

Chaoui of Morocco, 20 min., color, 1969. Universal Films.
$264.

Malawi, Two Young Men, 15 min., color, 1971. Churchill
Films, Inc., $170.
These two films can be used to show the spreading dissatisfaction and alienation that African high school graduates express when they are unable to find jobs or status in
society. Both are recommended for preview.

Leaving Home Blues, 51 min., color, 1971. N.B.C. Films.
$500, sale; $25, rental. A recent NBC-TV special concerning the movement of United States rural high
school graduates to urban centers in search of employment is now available in film. Teachers taking a thematic approach to worldwide social science phenomena
could use African and American examples.

Nomad Boy, 18 min., color, 1970. Association Films. Gratis
loan. The idealized version of education in the mind of
an African is shown. This UNICEF film is shot in Somalia. It is the only easily available film about this
country. Distributed on a free basis, long-range planning is necessary to obtain a print. When shown with
Malawi, Two Young Men, this film could start a class
unit on education and national development.

Tauw, 27½ min., color, 1971. Cokesbury Service Center,
$12, rental. Produced by Senegalese director Ousmane
Sembene. Shows the life of an unemployed young man
in Dakar, the capital city of Senegal, and is highly
critical of certain Islamic educational practices. One
should be very aware of the particular manner in which
the film depicts traditional Islamic institutions and
leaders. Americans with little knowledge of Islam's role

in western Africa may form damaging impressions.

WOMEN IN AFRICA

Teachers interested in feminism might want to attempt a cross-cultural study using American materials with those from Africa. An analysis of the many changing roles African women play in societies across the continent might be developed through the use of the following four films.

Films

Fear Women, 25 min., color, 1971. McGraw-Hill Film Division. $260, sale; $11, rental. Recommended for preview. Produced by UNESCO for N.E.T. It emphasizes the many new and changing economic and social roles of West African women.

A Forest People, the Mangbetu of the Congo, 11 min., B&W. 1935. Encyclopaedia Britannica. $170. Produced years ago, it continues to be commercially distributed. Viewer will see stereotyped roles of men and women. Father sits in his chair and is brought food by the children and mother who work, fish, and in general serve the male species.

Malawi, the Women, 20 min., color, 1971. Churchill Films. $170. Centers on the life-styles of three women in Malawi: a peasant farmer, an educated secretary, and a primary school-educated urban housewife.

Two Life Styles in West Africa, 17½ min., color, 1970. Bailey Films. $230, sale; $15, rental. A controversial film in many ways and one that might create new stereotypes. Using a dawn to dusk time sequence, the film shows a male farmer in his daily routine and a professional, female architect-builder in the capital city of Abidjan, Ivory Coast. In Western eyes, the status roles have been reversed. The woman dines on French cuisine at a hotel pool and following her lunch, goes water-skiing in the lagoon. The male works diligently in the fields and seems content with an ordered and successful family life in his village. Some viewers have commented that the film represents a subtle effort to illustrate the matriarchal supremacy idea in Black society. Others believe it represents the triumph of Western economic materialism over more traditional forms of social organization in the determination of new cultural values in Africa.

Other Resources

Contact the Foreign Student Adviser at your nearest college or university. It might be possible to secure the services of African women in a program or curriculum planning session.

Africa Report, July-August, 1972. Features an article on Africa's women. African-American Institute, 866 United Nations Plaza, New York, N.Y. 10017. $1.75.

The Women of Africa by Louise Crane. A recent book recommended for seventh- to twelfth-grade libraries. J.B. Lippincott, E. Washington Sq., Philadelphia, Pa. 19105. $4.95.

AFRICAN CULTURE

Art, Classroom Materials

Africa: Musical Instruments, Textiles, Jewelry and Carvings. Six filmstrips, six records. Warren Schloat. $84.

African Art and Culture. Three filmstrips, three records, and teacher's guide. Warren Schloat. $48.

African Arts. Monthly magazine highly recommended for school libraries. UCLA African Studies Center, University of California, Los Angeles, Calif. 90024. $8.

African Arts Study Kit. Kit consists of map of Africa (30 copies), African magazine filmstrip and teaching guide, Congolese art portfolio and teaching guide. Crowell Collier-Macmillan, School and Library Services, 866 Third Ave., New York, N.Y. 10022. $85.

African Culture Package. Five filmstrips on African creative culture, three artifacts, teacher reference book *African Kingdoms.* Time-Life Films. $65.95.

African Dress and Design. Twenty slides and teacher's guide. Society for Visual Education. $8.50.

Alva Museum Replicas. Unit 2/1: Africa the Glory of its Art. Unit 2/2: Africa Geography Tradition Culture. Contains replicas of artifacts, student activity programs (8 pages), a teacher's manual, color prints. Alva Museum Replicas, Inc., Education Division, 30-30 Northern Blvd., Long Island City, N.Y. 11101. Unit 2/1, $26; Unit 2/2, $35.

Discovering the Art of Africa. Twenty slides with explanatory notes. Society for Visual Education. $8.50.

Museum of Primitive Art. Set of twenty-five slides; no teacher's guide. Museum of Primitive Art. $15.

The Treasures and Traditions of African Art. Twenty slides and explanations. Society for Visual Education. $8.50.

Films

African Art and Sculpture, 21 min., color, 1971. Carousel Films. $250. Formerly a TV program in Philadelphia, this film offers introduction to various art forms.

The Anansi Tale, 8 min., color, 1970. Texture Films. $140, sale; $15, rental. Animated Ashanti, Ghana, traditional folktale, which is as useful in senior high as kindergarten for an introduction to the beliefs and spiritual background of an African people. Highly recommended for preview.

Arts and Crafts in West Africa, 10½ min., color, 1968. Bailey Film Associates. $135. Good introductory survey.

Cows of Dolo Ken Poye, 32 min., color, 1968. Holt Rinehart & Winston. $425. Resolving conflicts among the Kpelle, an African people in Liberia. Film is a cinema realité analysis of how a local conflict is adjudicated and solved. Designed for college anthropology courses, it is also useful in high school sociology or world culture courses.

Modern East African Wood Carver, 10 min., color, 1969. McGraw-Hill Film Division. $105, sale; $10, rental. An in-depth interview with a Tanzanian carver. Many responses indicate acute awareness of how commercialism of his work affects his spirit and creativity.

Art, Teacher References

African Art. Frank Willet. Excellent survey with 260 illustrations. Praeger Publishers, 111 Fourth Ave., New York, N.Y. 10003. 1971. $4.95. pap.

"Starting with the Arts" by Leon Clark, *Africa Report,* January/February 1973. A useful article, with both teaching suggestions and a film bibliography, about the work of Carolyn J. Maitland, a New York City high school art teacher. Back issues are available from *Africa Re-*

port, African-American Institute, 866 United Nations Plaza, New York, N.Y. 10017. $1.50 prepaid.

Music, Teacher References

Most large record stores have either copies of or access to British and French made records of contemporary African music.

Black Music of Two Worlds. John Roberts. Descriptions and analyses of African-American and African music styles of the New World and their relationships to African and European music. Designed for the general reader. Not wholly about music from the continent of Africa, the book takes a Pan-Africanist approach. Praeger Publishers, 111 Fourth Ave., New York, N.Y. 10003. 1972. $10.

Imported Records from Africa. African Music Center, 2341 Seventh Ave., New York, N.Y. 10030.

Literature, Teacher References

Reader's Guide to African Literature. Useful for finding additional information in magazines and books. Highly recommended for educators considering literary approach to the study of African culture. Provides a wealth of factually annotated analysis of materials. Africana Publishing Corporation, 101 Fifth Ave., New York, N.Y. 10003. 1972. $4.95. pap.

Record Catalog. Distributors of many traditional African recordings and folktales for children. Folkways/Scholastic Record Company, Englewood Cliffs, N.J. 07632.

6 *Africa and the world*

The study of Africa's relationships with the countries and problems of the contemporary world must begin with some knowledge of the colonial period and the factors that led to the attainment of independence by the new nations. If the teacher has covered Chapter Three, no further background study is needed. If students have not previously studied Africa's contact with Europe and the colonial conquest, however, the teacher is urged to familiarize himself with the information in Chapter Three and several of the sources recommended in order to acquire a brief background orientation. Many actions by the new African nations can only be understood in the light of the African reaction to European conquest, relations with the departing colonial power at the time of independence, and the eagerness modern Africans have shown to improve their position in a world dominated by European peoples.

This chapter is paired with the following one, which deals with Africa and the United States. For this reason African-American relationships will be covered very superficially here; American students should devote a special unit to how Africa affects affairs in their own country and how what America does affects the peoples of Africa.

It is suggested that students concentrate on a small number of countries in both units, as was recommended in the two units on nation building. Some attention needs to be given, however, to forces and patterns that apply to broad regions of Africa, because even though African nations have begun to differ from each other markedly in the area of foreign relations there are also some regional commonalities. It is extremely difficult to draw broad conclusions that have validity for all of Africa.

Foreign Policy Patterns at Independence

NATIONALIST IDEOLOGY

Widespread popular adherence to the ideology of African nationalism tended to produce certain views on foreign affairs that were common to most African states at the time of independence. These views did not always lead to similar policies, but the tendency toward similarity was clearly present. Students should discuss and understand the foreign policy tenets of African nationalism, since they form the ideological framework that most African leaders supported, at least in theory, during the early 1960s.

Avoidance of Foreign Entanglement. Just as the United States, upon achieving its freedom in the eighteenth century, declared that it must avoid being caught up in the intrigues, alliances, and power struggles of Europe, most Africans at the time of independence shared a feeling that they must avoid entanglement with the power struggles of the rest of the world.

Hostility to Foreign Interference. Closely allied to the fear of entanglement was a strong sensitivity to attempts by foreigners, individual or official, to influence Africa's internal or external affairs. Emerging from decades of powerful domination by colonial masters, Africans regarded any foreign interference as repugnant.

Nonalignment and Positive Neutrality. When African nations achieved independence, the main force in world affairs was the Cold War between the United States and the Soviet Union. Fearful of being involved on one side or the other, African nationalist ideology tended to support a position of nonalignment and neutrality. A few leaders, such as Kwame Nkrumah of Ghana, used the term "positive neutrality" to indicate that a neutralist view did not mean abdication of moral responsibility. According to this view, it was hoped that Africa might be able to help ease some of the East-West tensions.

African Unity. The nationalist ideology strongly favored unity among all African nations, so that they could cooperate with each other in the development of the continent for the benefit of all Africans. It also held that Africa's poverty and backwardness resulted, in part, from the fact that Europe had been able to "divide and rule," and argued that only a united stand by independent Africa could guarantee continued freedom from outside exploitation.

Third World Unity. It was also widely felt that Asia and Latin America, having also suffered from European exploitation and colonialism, were natural partners in misery. Although some Africans felt more strongly about this than others, there was a general profession of interest in developing closer communication and cooperation with Asia, the Middle East, and Latin America.

Expectation of Foreign Aid. Most African nationalists expected that foreign aid, in the form of grants, loans, technical assistance, investments, and trade, would flow into Africa in large amounts after independence. In part this was simple optimism and wishful thinking, but in part it reflected a deep nationalist feeling that the wealthy nations of the world (Europe and America) owed Africa massive assistance to compensate for the long period of exploitation and stagnation Africa had suffered under European domination.

Friendship with Former Colonial Powers. Despite the urgent pressure to throw off the yoke of colonialism and rid Africa of alien domination, the nationalist ideology was surprisingly free of deep hostility toward the departing colonial powers. Few African nations had to use military force or bitter confrontations to achieve political independence (Algeria and Guinea are notable exceptions), and most recognized the importance of the complex cultural and economic ties that remained at the time of independence.

POLICY SIMILARITIES FOLLOWING INDEPENDENCE

The wide adherence to African nationalism, added to the generally similar problems and conditions of most African nations at the time of independence, helped to produce a measure of similarity in actual foreign policies for the first few years after independence. (Differences, which have grown steadily since about 1960, are outlined in the next section.)

Relations with the Colonial Powers. With very few exceptions, most African nations entered into formal treaties of friendship and mutual assistance with the former colonial ruler. These treaties provided for continued or expanded trade, trade preference arrangements, encouragement of investments, continued grant and loan assistance, technical assistance, and mutual respect. In some cases (especially with the former French territories) the treaties also included provisions for military aid, but former British colonies tended to reject any provisions for African military support of Britain or for British military aid, beyond the continuation of some British officers and supplies.

The urgent financial needs of most new nations would have made it painful to cut off friendly relations with the departing colonial power. In addition, the economic links were so complex and deeply rooted that the economic systems of the new nations would have been paralyzed had they attempted to sever all ties.

Aid Policies. The severe underdevelopment and lack of indigenous capital made it essential that each independent nation shape its foreign policies in ways that would most effectively help to attract foreign aid. In the case of former British colonies, this resulted in overt, aggressive searches for expanded aid: establishment of relations with wealthy nations, friendship missions, encouragement of foreign investment, participation in international trade fairs, and the establishment of government agencies to pursue the search for foreign assistance.

In the case of former French colonies, which tended to retain close ties with France, the search for foreign aid was generally quieter and less obvious. This was partly due to jealous pressure from France, which regarded African involvement with other wealthy nations as a threat to French economic interests.

Active United Nations Participation. All African states quickly joined the United Nations after independence and placed high priority on active membership. They viewed the United Nations as a source of assistance in nation building and as a forum through which African interests in world affairs could be furthered without dangerous entanglements. As a result, African nations have become one of the largest blocs in the UN and meet regularly in an effort to coordinate their UN policies and activities.

Cautiousness in U.S.–U.S.S.R. Relations. While most African nations recognized the United States and the Soviet Union as important sources of trade and aid, they were reluctant to become enmeshed in the Cold War. Approaches to both nations tended to be cautious, although more so with the Soviet Union than the United States. This was due to several factors. The United States was more familiar to Africa, because of its close ties with Europe and its own long involvement in African affairs. During the 1950s the colonial powers permitted the United States to expand its trade relations and its assistance programs in Africa; they prohibited any Soviet involvement, on the other hand, even banning the importation of Soviet and Communist books in some territories.

Africans generally were fearful of communist expansionism and felt that they should develop relations with the Soviet Union slowly in order to understand better how to deal with it without allowing it to exert influence in African domestic affairs. As a general rule African nations, at the time of their independence, leaned toward the United States in many respects, even though it stopped short of aligning itself formally with the United States in the Cold War.

POLICY DIFFERENCES FOLLOWING INDEPENDENCE

Despite the above similarities in foreign policy, there were important differences that became manifest at the time of independence or within a very short period thereafter. As will be discussed in more detail later, these differences have grown steadily in the years since 1960, so that it has become very difficult to characterize African foreign policies without reference to individual countries or groups of like-minded countries.

Franco-British Differences. Britain and France adopted fundamentally different policies toward their colonies on the issue of independence. While both sought to maintain close and cordial relations and to insure that their economic interests would be protected, France chose to create a French community that would provide a strong, organic linkage among all its members. Most African colonies of France accepted this concept and became independent without severing all political ties with France.

Britain attempted to maintain close ties by encouraging former colonies to join the Commonwealth and to become independent dominions acknowledging the Queen as sovereign, on a status equal to that of Britain, Canada, Australia, and New Zealand. Most former colonies joined the Commonwealth and have remained within it but severed the tie to the throne by proclaiming themselves republics within a few years after independence. The Commonwealth is a more heterogeneous body than the French Community, with fewer requirements for homogeneous culture, economic relations, and other matters.

As a general rule, African states formerly under British rule have asserted their independence more aggressively than those under France. Such nations as Ghana, Tanzania, and Zambia have often taken firm positions on important world issues that are contradictory to those taken by Britain, while such nations as Ivory Coast, Senegal, Gabon, and Madagascar have frequently adopted positions similar to those of France.

Capitalist–Socialist Differences. As was noted in the chapters on nation building, virtually all African nations have espoused African socialism as a socio-economic philosophy, although definitions of this philosophy have differed. Some states have adopted policies that are clearly socialist, in that they involve state ownership of a large sector of production and strict limitations on private enterprise; examples are Guinea, Ghana under Nkrumah, Tanzania, and Zambia. Others have developed policies in which private enterprise is encouraged and state involvement is restricted to a few critical areas; examples are Ivory Coast, Gabon, and Malawi.

These differences reflect foreign policy orientations. The more socialistic states have nationalized some foreign-owned enterprises, have actively sought investments and trade with East as well as West, and have welcomed joint actions with like-minded nations in Asia and the Middle East. The more capitalistically oriented states have continued to seek foreign investments under liberal profit guarantees, have strengthened their ties with Western European economies, and have tended to be cool toward major socialist powers such as the Soviet Union and China.

Differences on African Unity. Even though the ideal of unity within Africa has long had widespread appeal, there have been important differences about how to achieve it. At one end of the spectrum have been such voices as Kwame

Nkrumah, who, when President of Ghana, strongly advocated a United States of Africa and used his influence persistently to try to bring African nations together under one banner to fight for economic emancipation from continuing ties with Europe and America.

At the other end of the spectrum have been such states as Ivory Coast, Liberia, and Malawi, which have insisted that African unity must be built very gradually, beginning with careful studies and conferences and emphasizing strictly limited measures such as inter-African trade agreements, new roads linking African states, and better communication networks within Africa.

Differences on Neo-Colonialism. Coinciding with the above differences at several points has been major disagreement within Africa over the concept of neo-colonialism and how to combat it. Most Africans agree that neo-colonialism is a force in Africa; they define it as a continuation of European economic control over Africa after political colonialism ended.

The nations and spokesmen who have been most vocal on neo-colonialism are those who have the most pronounced preferences for socialism and have avoided close ties with the West. Their view is that the Western world of Europe and the United States has bound Africa so closely economically that African development is virtually impossible except as the West doles out aid. Some have sought to counterbalance this economic dependence on the West by encouraging economic relationships with the Soviet Union and its allies; others (Tanzania being the prime example) have emphasized self-help and rural development, seeking aid from outside powers only for those areas of development that are essential and which cannot be managed by internal effort.

At the other extreme are spokesmen (Ivory Coast's President Houphouet-Boigny, for example) who recognize that neocolonialism exists but argue that Africa must deal with it by seeking development on the terms of Western capitalism. Those advocating this policy vigorously encourage foreign private investors, willingly negotiate preferential trade agreements, and welcome development in every sector of the economy that is of interest to investors. Believing that there is no alternative in the foreseeable future, they attempt to work within the Western economic system and to use it for their own purposes.

Of all the forces at work in the formation of foreign policy in the new African nations, those of an economic nature are generally the most important and the most complex. The teacher will recognize that this is an area of controversy for American schools, especially when a class is dealing with neo-colonialism and the reactions of Africa to it. Most Americans cherish the belief that their system of private enterprise is a good one. We expect that it will benefit other countries as well, and we find it difficult to accept that our economic relationships with underdeveloped areas such as Africa can be regarded as imperialist and exploitative. Yet not only do most Africans perceive themselves as being exploited by the economic policies of America and Europe (and, increasingly, the Soviet Union and its allies as well), there is substantial evidence that Africa's relative lack of progress is indeed caused by outside forces in the economic area.

Several of the references in the materials section deal forthrightly with this important topic as it is perceived by Africans and as it has been studied by scholars and international development specialists. It is strongly recommended that a class pay particular attention to this issue, in an effort to understand the deep, complex economic factors that are so influential in the formation of the foreign policies of African nations. Virtually every African government is sincerely concerned with attracting the funds, trade arrangements, and technical services needed to build its nation, but each tends to develop its own ways of going about this task depending on the beliefs of its leaders about what works. To some this means seeking close, friendly relations with one or a few European countries or the United States. To others it means trying to attract aid from the East to alleviate the present dependence on the Western economy. To still others it means forsaking foreign ventures, except in a few critical areas of need, and turning inward to try to build an internally viable economic and social system.

THE DEVELOPMENT OF PRAGMATISM IN FOREIGN AFFAIRS

The more than forty independent African states began their freedom from colonial rule with a number of similar beliefs and policies as well as some notable differences. As each has struggled with the intricacies of dealing with other countries on a sovereign basis, experience has accumulated and policies have evolved and been adapted in the light of this experience. Increasingly, African policies, both foreign and domestic, are formed pragmatically or on the basis of what seems to work; decreasingly, by ideological factors.

In the long run most authorities believe that this increasing pragmatism will result in sounder, more mature policies in African nations. In the short run, however, it seems destined to produce rapid policy changes that will not necessarily lead to progress. The military coups that have taken place in a number of African countries have often resulted in abrupt reversals of earlier policies. The new leaders attempt to better conditions by abolishing old policies and substituting a whole new set. This rapid swing of the pendulum of policy from one extreme to another is, in a sense, pragmatism at work, but it is rarely sound; a sensibly pragmatic process tends to work best by adding increments of experience and making modest changes in policy on the basis of accumulated experience.

Current Issues in African Foreign Affairs

While the growth of pragmatism inevitably brings more heterogeneity to African policies, there are a number of issues and problems that affect virtually all African nations. In response to these issues and problems each state finds it necessary to take positions and to behave in its relations with other countries on the basis of these positions.

The following outline of problems and issues is not exhaustive, but it includes those that most Africans regard as most important. It is suggested that the teacher lead the class in an examination of each, paying attention to what positions selected countries take; the factors that seem to have led each country to take the position it has; what factors might induce changes in policy; to what extent African positions might influence the outcome of each issue; and to what extent these problems are as important to other countries of the world as they are to Africa.

THE WORK OF THE UNITED NATIONS

Most African nations still regard the UN as a high priority and look to it as a forum to express their views, a potential means of resolving problems Africans regard as important, an alternative to entanglements with other countries on a bilateral basis, and a source of development assistance. African issues occupy much of the time of the General Assembly. Several great powers, including the United States, question whether the African role in the UN is valid; some argue that the small African nations are given a voice disproportionate to their population, wealth, and world importance.

WHITE DOMINATION OF SOUTHERN AFRICA

Most African countries maintain that no African can be truly free as long as White settlers and Portugal continue to dominate and oppress millions of Africans in Southern Africa. African pressure has kept Southern Africa in the foreground of UN debates for years.

A few years ago almost all African nations expressed similar views on Southern Africa, but there has been a tendency recently to adopt differing and conflicting positions. A few countries, such as Ivory Coast, Malawi, and Madagascar, have begun to favor a policy of dialogue with South Africa, which, they argue, might help to ease the restrictions under which that country's African population lives.

Most others, led by Algeria, Guinea, Tanzania, and Zambia, feel that South Africa's White government is too committed to its racial policies to be influenced by reasonable communication; these countries favor strong international action to force change in South Africa.

TRADE PROBLEMS

Since few African nations have well developed internal markets, they are heavily dependent on world trade and its fluctuating prices and tariffs. Most of Africa exports unprocessed agricultural and mineral products: cocoa, coffee, hides, grains, timber, ores, uncut gems, rubber, and fish. These products are processed, refined, and finished in Europe or the United States, and the final products are consumed largely outside of Africa. When prices fall or tariffs are high, African nations suffer rapidly and directly; they are extremely vulnerable to economic forces over which they have no control.

A major concern of foreign policies is to find ways of stabilizing prices and markets and obtaining low tariffs in order to maximize Africa's revenues and minimize fluctuations. This concern leads most African nations to seek trade agreements and treaties that bind them more closely to wealthy nations than they feel desirable, and to combine forces in such international bodies as the General Association on Trade and Tariffs (GATT) in order to increase their bargaining power. Despite energetic African efforts, however, most of the continent is still in a weak trade position, buffeted by market conditions and tariff policies too powerful for them to manipulate.

ACCESS TO CAPITAL AND DEBT PROBLEMS

The small size of the national product of every nation in Africa makes the formation of African capital reserves an extremely slow and difficult process. The only alternative, if economic and social development are to take place, is to seek loans (grants are very rare) from wealthier nations and such international agencies as the World Bank.

Loans are not always available on the terms and in the amounts desired by Africans; interest rates and repayment schedules are stiff. One result is that most African nations have become heavily in debt in the years since they gained independence and must devote an ever increasing amount of their national budgets to repaying loans. This has served to slow development since the ability to make new loans has declined as indebtedness has mounted. The earlier expectation that the wealthy nations of Europe and the United States would extend substantial aid to African development has disappeared, and Africans have realized that they must compete in the hard world of international finance, despite their poverty and economic weakness.

EUROPEAN ECONOMIC COMMUNITY

Although African nations generally prefer to stay as far removed from European affairs as possible, their heavy dependence on Britain, France, Germany, and other European nations for trade, loans, investments, and general economic matters has forced them to follow the development of the Common Market with interest. Most of the former French colonies have secured special relationships with the Common Market through their close links with France; other African nations have tended to look on the growth of the Common Market with skepticism or, in a few cases, have tried to negotiate special trade positions with it on an individual basis. Most African nations, however, agree that the growth of intra-European economic ties is important to Africa.

ORGANIZATION OF AFRICAN UNITY

Despite increasing divergence in African views on various foreign policy questions, the concept of African unity is sufficiently strong to insure that all African nations participate in the work of the Organization of African Unity (OAU). Frictions and disputes are present at OAU meetings, and many observers criticize its failures. Yet it is still supported by all Africa, and is rated favorably when compared to regional organizations in other parts of the world, such as the Organization of American States (OAS). Only the EEC (Common Market) is clearly more effective in binding together a number of countries in regional cooperation.

There are many problems within Africa that concern most African nations, in addition to that of racial oppression in Southern Africa, and the OAU is the main forum for discussions and attempts to solve these problems. Among the more important have been border disputes (e.g., between Ethiopia and Somalia, Kenya and Somalia, Morocco and Algeria), inter-African trade and tariff arrangements, and problems of minority ethnic groups and refugees. African states have on the whole agreed that African problems should be solved by Africans and regard the OAU, despite its weaknesses, as an appropriate agency within which to seek solutions.

REGIONAL COOPERATION

Most African nations have come to feel that the OAU is not the appropriate forum for building concrete associations for increased cooperation in trade, agricultural development, industrial development, and communication, except where it is clear that a continental approach is practicable. There is a widespread interest, therefore, in trying to build cooperative efforts among smaller groups of nations on a regional basis. Examples are the East African Community, the Senegal River States Association, the West African Council of the Entente, and a recently announced Nigeria–Togo economic association.

The French-speaking states have formed a number of large and small economic associations which have generally provided for increased cooperation in education, communication, transportation, and cultural matters as well as trade and economic cooperation. While these groups have not generally lasted for more than a few years, each time one has disbanded a new one has been formed to replace it.

Authorities agree that Africa's regional associations have failed to bring the strong ties of cooperation that they have been formed to achieve; the internal demands of each state's nation-building effort make it difficult to surrender enough sovereignty to insure substantial cooperation. Yet there remains a strong feeling among African leaders that only regional cooperation can enable the weak, underdeveloped states to build themselves into strong nations; despite failures, the efforts to build viable associations continue.

THE ARAB–ISRAELI CONFLICT

Africa tends to be drawn into this tense problem, for two reasons. First, many Africans are Muslims, and the nations of north and northeast Africa have affinities with the Arab world (Egypt and Libya play leading Arab roles). Second, Israel has maintained a strong and effective role in Africa, providing useful technical assistance and aid in economic development. The majority of African nations regard the

Arab–Israeli struggle with concern, even though their policies differ. Israel has successfully persuaded a number of African states to maintain a position of comparative neutrality when the problem has arisen in the United Nations, although few have been willing to place themselves squarely in support of the Israeli cause.

CHINA

In past years the United States has endeavored to influence African votes in the United Nations to support the claims of Nationalist China, while both Taiwan and Peking have sought direct African relationships and support. Gradually the African nations have shifted toward a pro-Peking attitude, which was greatly strengthened by the easing of American opposition to Peking's membership in the United Nations in 1971. Today few African countries maintain formal relations with Taiwan.

Some African nations feel that China is a natural ally and source of assistance since it is, like them, basically underdeveloped and struggling to modernize. In recent years Peking has encouraged this attitude by extending substantial economic and technical assistance to receptive African nations and by refraining from attempts to influence internal affairs in the nations with whom it has relations. No African nation has been interested in joining a Chinese power bloc, but there is a definite increase in cordial relations with China. Tanzania and Zambia, which have obtained massive Chinese aid in building a railroad linking the two countries, have developed especially good relations, although neither should be regarded as having placed itself under Communist Chinese influence.

AMERICAN RACIAL PROBLEMS

Most Africans follow American race relations with keen interest and have declared themselves sympathetic to the growth of Black Americans' rights and power. As with Southern Africa, however, each nation's policies tend to differ somewhat, and few have expressed opposition to the policies of the United States government on civil rights matters. (This question will be considered in Chapter Seven.)

LOW-PRIORITY PROBLEMS

Many problems which are considered troublesome by the United States and other non-African nations arouse little official concern in Africa. Although most Africans are unsympathetic to the American role in Southeast Asia, few African governments have expressed this in official policies. Similarly, Latin American affairs are rarely considered important to African interests (although several African states, such as Algeria, Guinea, and Ghana under Nkrumah have evinced sympathy with the Castro movement in Cuba, and Zambia maintains close communication with Chile, since the two are major world copper suppliers). As a rule African nations have taken no position or only mild positions on problems among European nations, preferring to remain uninvolved; for example, the Soviet intervention in Czechoslovakia, relations between East and West Germany, Northern Ireland, and Belgium's ethnic conflict. One major exception has been the North Atlantic Treaty Organization (NATO), which many Africans have criticized because of its inclusion and support of Portugal, the last European nation to control colonies in Africa.

A Note on Studying African Foreign Relations

The teacher is urged to devote proportionately more time to the African role in the United Nations and its specialized agencies than to a general survey of foreign affairs. Most of the above problems and issues concerning Africa are discussed within the United Nations, and most African nations prefer to deal with them there rather than on a bilateral basis. The materials section includes several references that provide good summaries and analyses of the African role within the United Nations, and there are excellent documents available from the United Nations itself.

The African preference for dealing with issues within the United Nations (and other bodies such as the OAU) stems partly from the high cost of maintaining competent diplomatic missions in a number of countries. Most African states maintain sizeable missions at the United Nations but restrict their other diplomatic posts to a few countries that are especially important, such as Britain, France, Germany, the Soviet Union, China, India, and the United States. In addition to the convenience of working within the United Nations, many African states feel that they can maximize their influence there by cooperating with each other or with other states on specific issues.

It will be noted that few newspapers or news magazines are recommended in the materials section. Even the best American publications carry very little coverage of African affairs and maintain few, if any, permanent staff in Africa. The result is that Africa is inadequately covered qualitatively as well as quantitatively. Scholars specializing in African affairs frequently deplore the scanty, erroneous articles on Africa in the American mass media and the frequency of biased interpretations. This means that students cannot rely on the mass media for a conventional current events study of African foreign affairs; they can use selected background articles and studies drawn from a variety of sources, including the only two American publications devoted to general African affairs: *Africa Report* and *Africa Today*.

Materials written by Africans are also extremely helpful, and a number are identified and recommended in the materials section. It is, of course, true that a proper understanding of any country's foreign policies can only be gained by knowing what that country's point of view is. This is especially true for Africa, because of the lack of familiarity and subtle stereotypes with which most non-Africans are handicapped in observing and analyzing African affairs.

Teaching Materials

Very few student materials are available for studying Africa's role in the international community. One immediate source of aid will be the Foreign Student Advisor at your nearest college or university. Through the advisor you should be able to make direct contact with an African student or faculty member in your community. If you live in or near a large urban area, you might also contact the local World Affairs Council. This organization and others like it arrange programs for African visitors. A final place where you might find Africans studying in America is at nearby seminaries or theological schools. Students can initiate these contacts.

TEACHER REFERENCES

Africa, the Politics of Unity. I. Wallerstein. Special emphasis given to efforts toward regional unity and international relations strategies of various African states. Random House, 201 East 50 St., New York, N.Y. 10022. 1970. $1.95.

Africa's Quest for Order. Fred Burke. Emphasis on nation-building ideas and systems, especially Chapters 6–7. "Spectrum" series. Prentice-Hall, Englewood Cliffs, N.J. 07632. 1964. $1.95.

Are You Going to Teach About Africa? Chapter 3: "African Paperback Texts, A Critical Review." Susan Hall. Contains an analysis of many paperback texts now on the market. Many of these texts have a chapter on Africa's role in the world. This booklet and chapter are recommended for curriculum designers. School Services Division, African-American Institute, 866 UN Plaza, New York, N.Y. 10017. 1970. $2.

Myth of Aid: The Hidden Agenda of the Development Reports. D.M. Goulet and M. Hudson. A strong critique of foreign assistance efforts stating that they do very little to effectively create greater prosperity for most Africans and serve essentially to promote the interests of donor states and governments in power. IDOC Books, 432 Park Ave. South, New York, N.Y. 10017. 1971. $2.95.

Political Awakening of Africa. R. Emerson and M. Kilson, eds. Historical growth to contemporary African political developments. Recommended as most useful introduction, especially Part 4. "Spectrum" series. Prentice-Hall, Englewood Cliffs, N.J. 07632. 1965. $1.95.

RESOURCES FOR STUDENTS AND EDUCATORS

Africa Report. A bimonthly magazine of contemporary African news and cultural activity. Recommended for library and social studies department resource center use. Contains education page specifically designed for K–12 African studies. African-American Institute, 866 United Nations Plaza, New York, N.Y. 10017. $9 for six issues.

New York Times. Every January the *New York Times* publishes an Africa supplement in one of its daily issues. The supplement emphasizes economic developments of the preceding year in a continental thematic and country-by-country style. The advertisements placed by businesses and African governments may be especially useful in analyzing international economic development in Africa. Write to the Circulation Manager, 201 West 43rd St., New York, N.Y. 10036.

Overseas Development Council, Suite 501, 1717 Massachusetts Ave., N.W., Washington, D.C. 20036. Pamphlets and short essays on foreign aid and development themes.

United Nations Development Project. African participation in the United Nations and its specialized agencies has led to a wide variety of UN projects in various African countries. Public Information Officer, 866 United Nations Plaza, Room 601, New York, N.Y. 10017.

United States Committee to UNICEF. Booklets and other information on UNICEF involvement in African development. Useful for showing objectives and key population groups in Africa creating and responding to development needs. Public Information Officer, 331 East 38th Street, New York, N.Y. 10017.

The World Bank Group. Information on development projects in Africa. Publishes annual reports and short descriptions of recently funded development schemes. 1818 H Street, N.W., Washington, D.C. 20433.

7 *Africa and the United States*

Americans generally agree that they know little about Africa and that they rarely understand the course of events on the continent. The "Dark Continent" stereotype is still to be dispelled from our minds. Yet surprisingly enough, there are long bonds of contact between Africa and the United States that have served to acquaint at least a few Americans with Africa and a few Africans with America. The task today is to expand these contacts and widen the circle of people in both lands who have some sympathetic understanding of life on the other continent.

The ties that have historically linked Africa and America stem from several points of contact:

The Slave Trade. Many hundreds of thousands of Africans were transplanted to the shores of the United States, and their descendants now number nearly 25,000,000. Some of these Afro-Americans have long maintained an active interest in their ancestral homeland, and the number who do so is growing rapidly today. Many aspects of African culture have influenced the development of American culture —in music, dance, foods, vocabulary, speech patterns, folklore, poetry, literature, and many other areas.

White Americans who engaged in buying and shipping

slaves came to know something of the life of Africa; some left records, which are still to be found in archives throughout the eastern United States. Africans learned something about America, too, both from these slave traders and from many Africans who regained their freedom and returned to Africa.

Maritime Traders. In addition to the slave traders, many American merchantmen were active in the trade along Africa's coasts from the mid-seventeenth century on. Even today cotton cloth is sometimes called "merikani" in Swahili, because so much of East Africa's cloth was bought from Yankee traders in the nineteenth century.

Missionaries. American missionaries became active in most parts of Africa during the nineteenth century and left a great legacy of conversion to Christianity and the founding of schools. Today large numbers of American churches continue mission work in Africa or maintain helpful fraternal relations with African churches of the same denomination.

Explorers. Although Henry Morton Stanley was the only American citizen to achieve international fame for his exploration (and exploitation) of Africa, dozens of other Americans helped to explore various parts of the continent, especially during the early nineteenth century: John Ledyard and Archibald Robbins of Connecticut and Paul du Chaillu of Philadelphia, for example. Many little known Americans undertook journeys of exploration that helped to identify some of the fabulous mineral deposits of southern Africa: John Hammond, Adam Renders, Frederick Barnum, and William Pickstone. Rees Davis helped introduce many commercial fruits into South Africa.

Political Relationships. Perhaps most important of all, Black

Americans have historically influenced the growth of liberation movements and Pan-Africanism in colonial Africa, and the modern force of independent Africa has influenced the course of the Black advancement movement in America. W.E.B. Du Bois, one of the founders of the National Association for the Advancement of Colored People, was also a founder of the Pan-African Congresses; Marcus Garvey's abortive but influential back-to-Africa movement served to focus African aspirations on Black advancement and the attention of Afro-Americans on their ancestral homeland.

Teachers who are approaching Africa with the relationship between Afro-Americans and Africa as a focus are urged to devote special attention to the diverse relationships that have existed between Africans and Afro-Americans for the past century and more and that have influenced developments in both Africa and the United States.

Africa's Importance to America

Despite the existence of the above historic ties between Africa and America, and much more extensive ties since World War II, Africa normally rates very low on the scale of American foreign policy priorities. The most cursory examination of American newspapers or documents on United States government budgets and world activities bears this out. Africa seems to become important only when there is some special crisis, such as the internal strife in the Congo (now Zaire) during the 1960s.

Yet Africa is important to America, and America is important to Africa. Five areas in which Africa is important to the United States can be identified for classroom attention:

1. Africa, though underdeveloped, is a major producer of many important ores and minerals (gold, diamonds, cobalt, uranium, manganese, oil) and is believed to have vast untapped resources. It offers a continually growing economic opportunity for America, as a producer of important raw materials and as a consumer of American manufactured goods. American investments in and trade with Africa are growing and are likely to continue to grow.

2. Africa's location gives it a strategic importance to both the United States and other world powers. When the Suez Canal is closed, oil and goods flow around the southern tip of Africa. The Indian Ocean has become an area of strategic interest to both the United States and the Soviet Union, making eastern Africa important for its harbors. Most of North Africa borders the Mediterranean, which is also of great strategic significance.

3. As the ancestral homeland of roughly twelve percent of the American people, Africa is slowly developing a symbolic importance paralleling that of Poland to Polish Americans, Ireland to Irish Americans, and Israel to Jewish Americans. Afro-Americans, who have historically maintained more interest in Africa than most other Americans suspected, are becoming increasingly concerned over the effects of American policies on developments in Africa. While they have not yet shown the intense partisanship that characterizes Jewish Americans' concern for Israel, their interest in Africa is clearly growing in the same direction.

4. In world politics, especially in the United Nations, the influence of African states is considerable and requires constant American attention. Even if Africa had no other importance to the United States, its voting power in the United Nations gives it special significance.

5. In the broader moral and political realm, America's position of world leadership requires it to maintain some concern about the underdevelopment and poverty of Africa. The entire non-European world has for many years watched the changing American role toward Africa as an index of American ability to live up to the inspiring ideals of American democracy. Until recent years there was widespread belief that America, because of her ideals of charity, freedom, and progress, would behave differently from other great powers. While that belief has been substantially eroded in the past decade, the peoples of the "have-not" countries of the earth still look to the United States for hope and help, if only because of its immense power and wealth.

Men of affairs question whether any state's policies are determined on purely moral or public relations grounds, and they argue that America has no moral obligation to help Africans relieve their underdeveloped state. Yet others argue that there are moral obligations that must shape the policies of any civilized nation as well as hard political and economic reasons why the affluent nations cannot stand aside while the majority of the world's people suffer poverty and relative stagnation. World conflicts, tensions, and wars, this view holds, frequently derive from the frustrations of peoples and states, and it predicts that the growing gap between the world's rich and poor nations will lead inevitably to future international problems.

Despite contemporary American apathy toward foreign aid, it is likely that America will develop a new sense of obligation toward the less affluent peoples of the world, either from a feeling of popular sympathy or from a recognition that peace for itself cannot be secure so long as the majority of the world lives in frustrated underdevelopment.

For many reasons Africa must figure prominently in this probable future renaissance of American responsibility as a world leader.

America's Importance to Africa

Just as it can be demonstrated that Africa holds considerable importance for America's future, Africa has long been influenced by the United States and will continue to be so in the future.

In the past, America's ideals inspired whole generations of African school children, who learned far more about George Washington, Abraham Lincoln, Thomas Paine, Thomas Jefferson, Booker T. Washington, W.E.B. Du Bois, and other Americans than we learned about African leaders. During the colonial era, the American Revolution and the struggles against slavery were powerful symbols to oppressed Africa. Africans supported the Allied cause during World War II, often inspired by the anti-fascist speeches of Roosevelt, Churchill, and other leaders.

As colonialism began to crumble following World War II, Africans tended to regard American beliefs in freedom and human dignity as a force in the anti-colonial movement. While subsequent events have weakened the African view of America as a nation motivated by noble ideals, many Africans still are aware of America's great heritage and expect our nation to become more helpful and sympathetic in the future.

Although Africans are primarily concerned to develop their own self-reliance, they often look on Black Americans as spiritual brothers and allies in a world in which Blacks tend to be dominated by Whites. They view the course of the civil rights movement in the United States as a portent of world civil rights progress, and they expect American Blacks, once they have achieved full political and economic equality, to act as a force for world Black advancement.

Africans are intimately influenced by America's actions, because of the tremendous power of American economic and political developments. If cocoa or coffee prices drop in the United States, the incomes of hundreds of thousands of Africans suffer; if copper prices go up in the American market, millions of Africans benefit. American support for a measure in the UN can powerfully affect the lives of African people, while American opposition can work just as powerfully in the other direction.

Because Africa's economic underdevelopment is its chief problem, the availability of American trade, investments, loans, and technical assistance are critical. Although other wealthy nations, such as Britain and France, are also crucially important to Africa, Africans are aware that America's economic influence is so extensive that even France and Britain feel its effects.

Post-Independence Developments in African-American Relations

It has been noted that there have been historic ties between the United States and Africa and that there are a number of reasons why Africa is important to America and vice versa. If one examines the trends in African-American relations over the past ten to fifteen years, there is a clear pattern characterized by a decline in African faith in America, a growth of pragmatism in the relationship, and numerous fluctuations in the degree of tension that has existed between African nations and the United States.

To assess contemporary events and better understand the possibilities for the future, the class should review the course of these developments.

THE INDEPENDENCE "HONEYMOON" PERIOD

As of approximately 1960, Africans tended to see America in terms of trust and hope, and Americans were rapidly developing a consciousness of "Africa emergent," which included a belief that the United States could and should help Africans to develop their new nations.

On the African side, America was viewed in terms of the ideals of the Revolutionary War, the anti-slavery struggle, the opportunities America afforded its immigrants, the American expressions of democratic values during World War II, and the generally pro-African stance adopted by the United States during the anti-colonial struggle. Africans expected the United States to become their major ally in their war against poverty and ignorance; they believed that American funds would flow in large quantities to help build roads, ports, schools, hospitals, and factories.

On the American side, Africa was seen as a land just throwing off an oppressive yoke, with its peoples emerging into the free world filled with aspirations and energies. There was a strong consensus among Americans that the wonders worked by the Marshall Plan in a war-crushed Europe could be repeated in Africa by a relatively modest application of American money and know-how.

Even though there were opposing minority voices in both

Africa and America, there was a strong expectation on both sides that the relationship would grow stronger.

THE KENNEDY–JOHNSON YEARS

During the presidency of John F. Kennedy, favorable feelings about Africa fostered the growth of aid programs and funds for African development. (American aid did not start under Kennedy; there was a steady growth from about 1950 on. But the peak years were between 1960 and 1965.) The Peace Corps was well received in most African countries, and a variety of other American agencies, public and private, stepped up their African activities.

During this period American students in much larger numbers than ever before began to study Africa, and the accent was on an optimistic view of the new Africa. African studies programs in American universities were created or greatly expanded. A widespread thirst for knowledge about Africa was evident in both educational institutions and public circles.

American support for African independence reached its height during the early 1960s. As each new country gained its freedom (seventeen became independent in 1960 alone), the United States hailed it and expressed warm wishes for its future prosperity and advancement. There was widespread American expectation that the movement for African freedom would sweep the entire continent, eventually ousting Portugal from its colonies in Angola, Guinea, and Mozambique, and wresting control from White minorities in Namibia (South-West Africa), Rhodesia, and South Africa. Most Americans expected Africans to control their own affairs and welcomed this control as a desirable step toward human freedom and dignity.

The trend toward pro-African sympathies and the growth of American aid were widely acclaimed in Africa, and most African countries based their policies, at least in part, on the development of close relations with the United States. Even those countries, such as Ghana and Guinea, that had pronounced policies of steering a neutral course between the United States and the Soviet Union welcomed the growth of American interest and assistance and sought to encourage maximum American aid, trade, and investment.

Just as Americans tended to be optimistic, even naive, in their expectations about Africa, so Africans tended to expect a great deal from the United States and Americans. Americans were greeted warmly and hospitably. African diplomatic and trade missions traveled to the United States in large numbers, anticipating a warm reception and expanded American assistance.

By 1965 it was possible to discern a trend away from these warm views, by both Africans and Americans, and the growth of a less naive, less charitable, more pragmatic relationship. The development of the new relationship was not smooth and painless, however. Bitter tensions occurred, leaving feelings of hostility and recrimination in their wake.

AMERICAN AID PROGRAMS

One factor in the changed relationship was the outcome of the American assistance program to various African countries. From the African point of view, it was never large enough. After achieving a maximum amount of about $2.677 billion in 1966, aid declined slowly. Countries received aid unequally, since the United States tended to channel more assistance to those countries whose policies it preferred (or those it hoped to influence), whose strategic position it believed more important, or whose economic potential it believed greatest.

American official and philanthropic aid carried strings, even though most of the strings were administrative rather than political: the United States insisted on helping plan projects, it required that most of the aid money be spent on American goods and services (even though they were more expensive), and it watched the expenditure of its aid funds with a closeness that Africans often viewed as excessive and meddlesome. Further, American aid went into those areas it believed most important, even though Africans may have preferred to use it for other purposes.

American observers and development assistance experts gradually came to doubt the efficacy of their aid. They often felt that Africans were inefficient in development projects and that their political leaders were inept in management. Even where individual assistance projects seemed to prosper, they did not seem to effect the widespread social and economic development that both Africans and Americans wanted. Many Americans began to believe that the majority of Africans were not willing to make the changes and sacrifices necessary for national development but instead expected foreign aid to transform their nations without local effort.

By 1970 few African countries were making the energetic efforts to secure American aid that they had a few years earlier. Most continued to accept aid willingly, and many sought American funds or expertise for specific projects (such as Botswana's new copper-zinc mining development), but overall, Africa had come to see that the United States was not an unlimited source of aid. Some states had come to feel that it was by no means the best source of aid. America, in turn, continued to reduce its budget for aid to Africa as well as its expectations of what aid programs could achieve.

THE EASING OF THE COLD WAR

Although neither Africans nor Americans emphasized it during the early 1960s, one factor in the American support for Africa was the belief that communism might spread there unless the United States established itself first. There was intense rivalry between the United States and the Soviet Union between about 1958 and 1966, each using aid to Africa as a major weapon. By 1965–1966 both great powers had learned that aid did not buy friendship in Africa, where there has continued to be strong distaste for foreigners who attempt to influence African affairs. The result was a gradual leveling off and decline in both the rivalry and the expenditures on development assistance for Africa.

To a large extent Africa has been neutral in the East-West rivalry, partially because of the reluctance of Africans to align themselves to any world power bloc. One result, however, has been less interest on the part of either the United States or the Soviet Union to outdo the other in providing massive development assistance.

AMERICAN POSITIONS ON AFRICAN PROBLEMS

Since 1960 several serious conflicts have erupted in Africa about which the United States has taken positions that have incurred the hostility of some African nations. The first such crisis was that in the Congo in 1960; the majority of Africans clearly disapproved the American lack of support for

Patrice Lumumba, and this disapproval was only partly compensated for by the support of the central government when Katanga tried to secede. Similarly, American actions during the Nigerian civil war, in which the United States officially supported the federal government but private Americans assisted Biafra, aroused some hostility in Africa, especially in Nigeria.

Perhaps the most disturbing incident was that of the United States airlifting Belgian troops to protect the 2,000 Europeans in Stanleyville during the Congolese civil war; Africans almost unanimously regarded this action as a symbol of American lack of faith in African responsibility and as an arrogant interference in the internal affairs of an African nation.

By far the most persistent cause of tension, however, has been the continuing American unwillingness to take significant action to alleviate the plight of the oppressed African majority in Southern Africa. Many Africans believe that the United States is guilty of racism in this situation, since the oppressed peoples are Black; if the oppressed group were White, Africans argue, the United States (and Europe) would long ago have taken effective measures to enforce change.

American positions on African problems have naturally not been universally unpopular among Africans; on each occasion some Africans have applauded the United States stand. Africans are rarely unanimous on problems themselves. The net effect of the past decade has been the erosion of the earlier African faith in the rightness of America, in effect removing the United States from a pedestal and placing it alongside other nations, which act largely in accord with self-interest.

AMERICAN VIEWS OF AFRICAN LEADERS

Many Africans are intolerant of outside criticism especially if the criticism comes from White Americans or Europeans. For this reason there has been a certain adverse reaction to the American tendency to categorize noted African leaders as good or bad, especially as regards their stands on East–West issues. Americans (influenced heavily by the American mass media) have tended to regard certain African leaders as pro-communist: Nkrumah, Nyerere, Kaunda, Nasser, and Touré. Africans often resent such categorical judgments by foreigners and point out that each of these men has followed very different policies from the others on East–West issues as well as on domestic affairs. Nyerere and Kaunda are particularly popular in Africa as staunch advocates of African independence who would never surrender the freedom of their countries to any foreign power, East or West.

GOVERNMENTAL DEVELOPMENTS IN AFRICA

In the past decade many developments in Africa have diminished American confidence and faith in Africa. The numerous coup d'etats and changes in government, the number of countries that have made internal political opposition difficult, and the widespread nationalization of foreign and private industries have all been unfavorably regarded by most Americans.

In sharp contrast to the popular goodwill toward Africa of the early 1960s, there is now a prevalent view that Africans are somewhat undemocratic, that their governments are unstable, and that they have little respect for contracts and the role of foreign investors. Needless to say, Africans have their own justifications for such measures as one-party political systems and nationalization of essential industries. Some Americans understand and appreciate the African view of these matters; many more Americans, however, have developed a rather negative view of African actions in the past decade.

Contemporary African–American Relations

The diminution of the "honeymoon" attitudes in Africa and America and the effects of various developments over the past decade have brought about new relationships that some observers describe as "normal," others as "unsatisfactory." However they may be categorized, they are more complex now than ten years ago. One must now examine American relations with each African country individually, since American relations with some (Liberia, Ethiopia, Botswana, Tunisia) are at the moment quite good and with others (Tanzania, Zambia, Libya) clearly less intimate than previously.

Several factors that are important in influencing relations between the United States and African countries are outlined here. One, that of the attitudes and actions of Afro-Americans, is so important for American students to understand that it is treated separately and in more detail than the others at the end of the chapter.

THE GENERAL LOW PRIORITY OF AFRICA

As a general rule, almost all American institutions, government and private, accord African affairs a relatively low priority, compared with ten years ago or with other parts of the world such as Europe or Indochina.

United States Government. Current United States government policies (both Democrat and Republican) tend to assign Africa low priority. Aid funds for Africa continue to diminish as they do for most of the underdeveloped world, and Africa's relative position, compared with Asia, Latin America, and the Middle East, is slightly poorer now than a few years ago. It is only when a major conflict occurs, e.g., the Nigerian civil war, that the United States government temporarily pays greater attention to African affairs.

Private Industry. Private industry is notably cautious in its attitudes toward foreign trade and investments, especially in the underdeveloped lands; it tends to trade and invest where there are substantial prospects of profits, low risks, and maximum freedom of operation. Africa has never been as attractive to American industry as Canada, Europe, and Latin America, except where potential profits seemed worth the risk: copper in Zambia and Zaire, copper-zinc in Botswana, bauxite in Ghana and Guinea, and oil in Libya, Nigeria, and Angola.

Today American investment in Africa is increasing, but slowly and cautiously. Africa's investment attractiveness to America, in comparison to that of other parts of the world, is still relatively low and shows no sign of improving at present. American funds invested in Africa comprise less than five percent of the total United States foreign investment.

Private Philanthropy. The large American charitable trusts and foundations today spend a smaller proportion of their funds on African research and assistance than was the case a few years ago. As a general rule, they have shifted from international concerns toward domestic ones, arguing that their limited funds can accomplish more on social and medical projects in the United States than on trying to help with the massive problems of the underdeveloped world.

Schools and Colleges. American education is facing a general financial crisis, and in efforts to economize, schools and colleges have tended to reduce expenditures on African studies. There is still a trend toward more study of the non-Western world in elementary and high schools, with Africa importantly included, but the growth of specialized study of Africa has slowed markedly.

Public Apathy. American public opinion has shifted away from international to domestic problems during the past few years, due to growing concern over domestic tensions, disillusionment with the United States role in Asia, and a vague feeling that American involvement abroad has not accomplished its objectives. Africa, whose dozens of small nations are weak and unlikely to cause difficulties for the United States, has tended to seem less immediate and important to the general public. Many Americans are confused about events in Africa, especially coups and apparent instability. It is a human tendency to ignore difficult problems if they seem to have little immediate effect on individuals not involved in them.

POSITIVE FORCES

Despite waning American interest and assistance to Africa, there are several organizations that maintain contact and remain involved.

Liberal Institutions and Individuals. There are many organizations that devote all or part of their work to Africa; they generally feel that Africa is not accorded its just share of American interest and help. To name only a few, one might cite the African-American Institute, American Committee on Africa, CARE, Catholic Relief Services, National Council of Churches, American Field Service, and Church World Service.

Numerous Black American political and civil rights groups have proclaimed African affairs important to America.

Academic Groups. There are scholarly and academic groups that are similarly devoted to African affairs: the African Studies Association, the African Heritage Studies Association, and African studies centers at such universities as Boston University, Northwestern University, University of California at Los Angeles, Indiana University, the University of Wisconsin, and Howard University.

Business Firms. Many American business firms that have substantial investments in Africa, or conduct trade with Africa, maintain close contact with African developments. There is an active African-American Chamber of Commerce in New York, and business executives hold many meetings and discussions with each other and with African business and governmental leaders.

United States Government Interests. In Congress a relatively small group of Representatives and Senators, both Black and White, follow African affairs with some sympathy and informed interest. Their number is small; less than fifty manifest a continuing, active interest in Africa. In the United States government, especially in the Department of State, the Agency for International Development, the U.S. Information Agency, and the U.S. Office of Education, there are small cadres of specialists who are generally sympathetic to African problems and argue for a sustained United States involvement in African assistance efforts.

NEGATIVE FORCES

On the more conservative side, there are other organizations that either work to deemphasize American contact with Africa or that tend to influence policies on Africa in the opposite direction from the above positive forces.

Conservative Political Groups. A few groups of a conservative nature, such as the American African Affairs Association and the Friends of Rhodesia, maintain an active interest in Africa. In general they are sympathetic to the interests of South Africa, Portugal, and Rhodesia and are critical of developments in independent Black Africa. Aligned with these groups and individuals are various staunchly conservative newspapers and magazines.

Business Interests. Although relatively few firms adopt an overtly anti-African position, many businessmen tend toward conservative attitudes on African issues and are favorably inclined toward White interests in Southern Africa. This is especially true of firms and executives that have large business involvements in Southern Africa. Viewing African affairs from the standpoint of ease of doing business, security of investment, and antipathy toward policies of nationalization of industry, many United States businessmen are skeptical of developments in independent Black Africa. They tend to emphasize the existence of corruption, governmental instability, inefficiency, and disrespect for private investments in Black Africa; they contrast White-ruled Southern Africa favorably by the same criteria.

United States Government Interests. Congress includes a group of Representatives and Senators, again numbering no more than about fifty, who follow African affairs regularly and influence policy in a conservative direction.

In the Department of State, the Defense Department, and other agencies there are cadres of officials who tend to deemphasize the importance of Africa to the United States. Frequently individuals in this category argue that United States ties with Portugal in NATO outweigh the need to placate Black Africa by criticizing Portugal's colonial role in Africa, that the strategic need for chrome outweighs the obligation of the United States to support the UN program of economic sanctions against Rhodesia, and that South Africa's military strength makes it a useful ally in the struggle against world communism.

Africa and Black America

It is often noted that America's 25,000,000 citizens of African descent make the United States the third largest African country in the world (after Nigeria and Brazil) and the wealthiest in terms of per capita income. A few decades ago it seemed apparent that the vast majority of these transplanted Africans had irrevocably lost any identification with their kin in Africa, were committed to total absorption into American society and culture, and rejected their African heritage as being somehow primitive and demeaning.

Today there are many indications that this rejection of

Africa, which was never as deep or extensive as White Americans believed, is rapidly giving way to a new pride in the African heritage and a keen interest in contemporary African-American relations.

Students who want to understand Africa and African-American relations should spend enough time on this phenomenon to appreciate its growing strength and its logical appeal to many Black Americans. Only a few years ago White Americans believed that African-American relations could be studied without reference to the African-Afro-American relationship. Over the next few decades, however, this relationship is going to be a vital factor in the larger relationship between the United States and African countries, and it cannot be ignored.

HISTORICAL TIES

For the sake of completeness, it is desirable to outline briefly the kinds of ties between Africa and Afro-Americans that were never fully extinguished by the conditions of slavery and the African diaspora.

Many Black American families maintained a tenuous sense of continuity and family heritage that included some information, often very vague, about African origins and the conditions under which original slave ancestors had been enslaved. Even though information was imprecise, many young Afro-Americans, from the seventeenth century to today, have dreamed about their African ancestry, even fantasizing (as many White youngsters have done) that they might have been descendants of nobles or great warriors.

Even where genealogical information was absent or erroneous, the African heritage often persisted in the form of recipes of special dishes, tunes and dances, folktales, nick-names, family relationships, and attitudes about life. The contemporary interest in "soul culture" reflects the reality of an Afro-American culture, which is a blend of the dominant American culture and that of African ancestors.

Black Americans in significant numbers visited Africa during the eighteenth and nineteenth centuries as seamen, traders, adventurers, missionaries, and educators. The African Methodist Episcopal Church and others were re-sponsible for educating surprisingly large numbers of Africans and for bringing a trickle of young Africans to Tuskegee, Lincoln, and other Black institutions for higher education.

The establishment of Liberia by freed slaves and White philanthropists in the early nineteenth century created a tie that has remained strong for more than a century. Literally thousands of Afro-Americans and Liberians have visited each other, exchanged letters, intermarried, and perpetuated a tie between Africa and America.

Black intellectual and political activities of the nine-teenth and twentieth centuries have often united Afro-Americans with Africans in Africa, in the Caribbean, and in Europe. The struggle for African freedom has long been a unifying theme for Black thinkers, poets, writers, and political activists. Garvey, Du Bois, Williams, Padmore, and scores of others have served as links.

The struggles for Black advancement and African free-dom have, of course, never been a totally coordinated, united front movement. Men from various African coun-tries, the United States, the West Indies, and other areas have naturally concentrated their energies on the struggle in their own country of birth. They have often disagreed and at times have worked at cross purposes. Yet there has been a thread of unity and of shared ideas and aspirations, which is still a force in both Africa and America.

MODERN DEVELOPMENTS

The Degree of Unity. Much controversy surrounds the question of the extent to which Africans identify with Afro-Americans and the latter with Africans. It is not difficult to give evidence that there is disunity, but there is also evidence of unity. In the materials section are references that will help students examine the evidence and arguments, both pro and con. The teacher is reminded that this matter, like most, is one on which no two individuals adopt precisely the same position; this is especially true in studying the deeply rooted attitudes of Africans and Afro-Americans on the emotionally tinged issue of Black unity. Some individuals, on both continents, are almost totally committed to racial unity at all costs, others find the concept repugnant, and most are somewhere between the extremes. Whatever degree of unity exists, it is well to remember that it is in a process of change and that its rate of change varies greatly depending on the different circumstances that make Black unity more or less urgently perceived. It is clear that the unity sentiment is growing rapidly among Afro-Americans, along with their increasing insistence on full rights and power in American society.

The African Heritage Movement. All Americans are familiar with the growth in recent years of popular Black interest in African-ness—the Afro hair style, the wearing of beads and dashikis, the adoption of African names, and the demand for African courses, including African languages, in American schools. While some of this may be a temporary fad, it is rooted in a growth of pride in race and heritage. Because of this growth, both White and Black American students would do well to learn more about Africa and the influence of its heritage in America.

Black Activism in Politics. Again all Americans are familiar with the resurgence of Blacks in political movements, both within and outside of the major political parties. Virtually all Black political leaders have spoken publicly on African questions, generally calling for more American attention to Africa, more technical assistance, and, especially, a more aggressive stand against the oppression of Africans in Southern Africa. One of the largest all-Black demonstrations in our nation's history took place in Washington on African Liberation Day, May 25, 1972.

There has been a pronounced growth of Black leadership in the past few years in the liberal organizations that manifest interest in African affairs. Several groups, such as the African Heritage Studies Association and the Interreligious Foundation for Community Organization, have adopted strong African programs under Afro-American leadership.

White Reaction. Just as many White Americans have been surprised and apprehensive at the rapid growth of Black power movements and demands on the domestic scene, they are often uneasy at the growing identification of Black Americans with Africa. Some seem to suspect that Black unity is pointedly anti-White and dangerous to racial harmony in the United States.

This is a question American students should examine openly—it is one of the phenomena of our times, and it is an essential aspect of the African-American relationship. Many Afro-Americans see links with Africans as helpful to their struggle, and they feel that American policy toward Africa is a legitimate area for their concern. This will grow over the next few years. Just as Jewish-Americans seek openly to insure a friendly United States policy toward Israel, Afro-Americans are coming to demand a more favorable policy on African questions. While it is impossible to predict the specific channels this growing Black interest in African policy will take over the next ten to fifteen years, it will increase and will become a normal force in the American political process.

Teaching Materials

TEACHER REFERENCES

Africa and United States Policy. R. Emerson. A survey of United States relationships with Africa since 1945. Primarily reflects official United States Government and commercial relationships. Out of print but available in many libraries. "Spectrum" series. Prentice-Hall, 1967. pap.

Americans in Black Africa up to 1865. 1964. $1.50. *Americans in Africa 1865–1900.* 1966, $3. P. Duignan and C. Clendenen. Useful historical surveys with extensive bibliographies; also useful student reading, grades 10–12. Hoover Institute Studies, Stanford University, Stanford, Calif. 94305.

The Great Powers and Africa. Waldemar Neilsen. A post-World War II description and analysis of British, French, and American relationships with African states and peoples. Emphasizes government-to-government and international organizations' policies. Recommended as teacher background for senior high government or world history courses. Praeger Publishers, 111 Fourth Ave., New York, N.Y. 10003, 1969. $11.95.

Inside America: A Black African Speaks Out. Fred Qwesi Hayford. The first book ever written by an African about the United States for the American market. Acropolis Books, Colortone Bldg., 2400 17th St., N.W., Washington, D.C. 20009. 1972. $6.95.

Also refer to History Teaching Materials on the Trans-Atlantic slave trade at the end of Chapter Three.

AFRO-AMERICAN-AFRICAN RELATIONSHIPS

Apropos of Africa, Sentiments of Negro American Leaders on Africa from the 1800's to the 1950's. Adelide Hill and Martin Kilson, eds. A highly recommended collection of documents useful for teachers of American history as well as of African studies and Afro-American history. A "one of its kind" book. Humanities Press, 450 Park Ave. South, New York, N.Y. 10016. 1968. $12.

Edward Wilmot Blyden, Pan-Negro Patriot. H. Lynch. Biography of an early pan-Africanist, important in the history of Liberia and the development of Black intellectual philosophy. Oxford University Press, 200 Madison Ave., New York, N.Y. 10022. 1971. $1.95. pap.

The Ideological Origins of Black Nationalism. Sterling Stuckey. An analysis of nineteenth-century Black American thoughts about and policies toward establishing an independent nation. Beacon Press, 25 Beacon St., Boston, Mass. 02108. 1971. $8.95.

Roots. Alex Haley. A story of a successful search by an

Afro-American for his family roots in West Africa. Doubleday, Garden City, N.Y. 11530. To be published. Alex Haley has also created the Kinte Foundation to continue genealogical research into the African origins of Black Americans. 716 National Press Bldg., Washington, D.C. 20004.

Search for a Place, Black Separatism and Africa, 1860. M.R. Delaney and R. Campbell. Account of the visit of two Afro-Americans to West Africa in 1859–1860. May be used as primary resource material in teaching about pre-colonial African societies. University of Michigan Press, Ann Arbor, Mich. 48106. 1971. $2.25.

UNITED STATES GOVERNMENT SOURCES OF INFORMATION

Agency for International Development. Ask for AID Program in Africa information. Public Information Office, Africa Section, Department of State, D Street and 22nd St., N.W., Washington, D.C. 20402.

Department of Commerce. Ask for information on United States-African trade. Useful to show extent of United States private interest in Africa. 14th between E and Constitution Ave., N.W., Washington, D.C. 20230.

Peace Corps. Ask for general information on African projects and application forms. Information can illustrate African-defined areas of development. Application forms useful to show students skills needed in development process. 806 Connecticut Ave., N.W., Washington, D.C. 20525.

United States and Africa in the 70's. Department of State Publication 8523, African series 48. Policies of the

Nixon Administration in Africa. Office of Media Services, Bureau of Public Affairs, Government Printing Office, Washington, D.C. 20402. $.25. pap.

MAGAZINES

African Progress. Africa Investors and Placement Service, Inc. 172 Madison Ave., New York, N.Y. 10016. Monthly, $10.

Black America. 24 W. Shelten Ave., Philadelphia, Pa. 19144. Twelve issues, $10.

Black World. Johnson Publishing Company, 1820 South Michigan Ave., Chicago, Ill. 60616. Monthly, $5.

Black Scholar. Black World Foundation (a nonprofit educational organization), P.O. Box 908, Sausalito, Calif. 94965. Ten issues, $10.

Drum and Spear Press Publications. These books, pamphlets, and children's educational materials specialize in African, Afro-American, and Pan-African journalism. Write for catalog at 1802 Belmont Rd., Washington, D.C. 20009.

Encore. 572 Madison Ave., New York, N.Y. 10022. Monthly, $8.

Essence. Box 2989, Boulder, Colo. 80302. Monthly. $5.

Sepia. 122 Harding St., Fort Worth, Tex. 76102. Monthly, $6.

FILMS

(See Appendix for producers' addresses.)

The Adventurer Returns, 30 min., color, 1968. McGraw-Hill.

$425, sale; $35, rental. For an African view of American society, this film is highly recommended. Story concerns a group of rural African youth in Niger and their efforts to terrorize a village following their adoption of American cowboy attire and behavior. For educators in charge of in-service education. This film will get participants' attention and get your workshop rolling. The most unique film available.

Africa's Gift, Two reels, 28 min. each, color, 1973. Westinghouse Learning Press. $600, sale; $60, rental. This film was originally a television production. It is most valuable for a senior high school or adult audience. Operating at two levels, it is highly recommended for educators who want to show the definite links between West African rural art and music and contemporary art and music in the Americas. African instruments are shown with quick transition to Mongo Santamaria's Afro-Cuban music and Lionel Hampton's jazz. The linkage is immediately seen and heard. African influences on the art of many famous European and American artists are clearly shown. Numerous ritual dances and art works of West African peoples are shown. Students will have to be previously prepared to fully understand the function of art, ritual dance, and music in these African societies. The best film available showing linkage between cultures of the Americas and West Africa.

Negro Art Festival, Dakar, Senegal, 20 min., color, 1965. McGraw-Hill. $180, sale; $11, rental. Filmed record of the 1964 Pan-African cultural conference.

Omuwale, 30 min., B&W, 1965. NET, various university film libraries for rental. Experiences and reactions of an African-American returning to West Africa. A personal portrayal of one man's efforts to better understand himself and establish his identity as an American with an African heritage. Recommended for grades nine through twelve.

Our Future with the Third World, 26 min., B&W, 1970. Holt, Rinehart and Winston, Inc. $180. James Foreman and Imamu Baraka (LeRoi Jones) outline the relationship of Afro-Americans to Africa. Emphasis on historical links and possibilities of unified Pan-African political action in the United States, Africa, and international relations.

We: An African People, 45 min., color, 1970. Senegal Productions. $450, sale; $125, rental. Film record of the Pan-African Cultural Festival in 1970 in Algiers, Algeria. "Produced, directed, written, filmed by Black people." Highly recommended visual record of musical, artistic, dance extravaganza.

AMERICAN ORGANIZATIONS
WITH AFRICAN PROGRAMS

Teachers can obtain general information from these organizations that may be used to develop an analysis of United States-African relationships. Students can also write and present the class with their analyses of a single organization and its objectives in working with Africans.

African-American Chamber of Commerce, 99 Church St., New York, N.Y. 10007. A who's who of United States investors in Africa.

The African-American Institute, 866 United Nations Plaza, New York, N.Y. 10017. Sponsors African and American student scholarship programs, visitor and travel projects, and a wide range of educational services to Americans interested in Africa.

African Studies Association, Shiffman Center, Room 218, Brandeis University, Waltham, Mass. 02154. Academic scholarly organization whose membership, programs, and publications will be useful to educators.

American Field Service, 313 East 43rd St., New York, N.Y. 10017. Student exchange programs and small-scale economic development efforts in Africa.

African Heritage Studies Association, % Africana Studies & Research Center, Cornell University, 310 Trithammer Rd., Ithaca, N.Y. 14850. A membership group dedicated to scholarly research and Black cultural and political mobilization on a Pan-Africanist basis.

CARE (Cooperative for American Relief Everywhere), 660 First Ave., New York, N.Y. 10017.

Catholic Relief Services, 350 Fifth Ave., New York, N.Y. 10001.

Church World Service, 475 Riverside Dr., New York, N.Y. 10027.

The Committee of People of African Descent in America, 475 Riverside Dr., Room 576, New York, N.Y. 10027. CPADA is engaged in mobilizing Black people in the Americas to aid their brethren in Southern Africa.

Crossroads Africa, Inc., 150 Fifth Ave., New York, N.Y. 10011. Travel and development programs in Africa.

Institute of International Education, 809 United Nations Plaza, New York, N.Y. 10017. Administers exchange and scholarship programs.

Maryknoll Missions, Maryknoll, New York 10562.

National Committee of Black Churchmen, 40 East 125th St., Room 503, New York, N.Y. 10035. Has an Africa

Commission engaged in Pan-African political and social mobilization.

National Council of the Churches of Christ in the U.S.A., 475 Riverside Dr., New York, N.Y. 10027. Overseas Mission Board active in many African countries.

Opportunities Industrial Council, 1225 North Broad St., Philadelphia, Pa. 19122. OIC works with African governments to assist them in urban manpower training and economic development.

Phelps-Stokes Fund, 297 Park Ave. South, New York, N.Y. 10010. Assists African students in United States.

8 The dilemma of Southern Africa

Southern Africa is a group of ten countries that occupy the southern portion of the continent. Five are independent nations ruled by African governments, and five are states with African majorities who are ruled by European settler governments or colonial powers.

The five independent nations are Botswana, Lesotho, Malawi, Swaziland, and Zambia. Of these, Lesotho is entirely surrounded by the Republic of South Africa, with its White government; Swaziland is lodged between South Africa and the Portuguese colony of Mozambique; and Botswana is surrounded by South Africa and White-ruled Namibia, except for a tiny border strip with independent Zambia. Only Malawi and Zambia have extensive borders contiguous to free African nations.

The five states in which the majority African populations are ruled by racial minorities or colonial power are Angola (Portuguese), Mozambique (Portuguese), Namibia (often called South-West Africa and controlled by South Africa), the Republic of South Africa, and Rhodesia. Rhodesia is legally a colony of Britain, but its small (250,000) White settler population rules virtually independently.

Many authorities feel it is useful to consider an eleventh

country, Guinea (Bissau), a Portuguese colony in West Africa, along with the ten southern territories, since its status and problems are so similiar to those of Angola and Mozambique.

It is very important to recognize that all the countries of Southern Africa form a unit, despite their differences. The five that are ruled by elected Black governments are influenced, to one degree or another, by the great economic and communications power of South Africa, Rhodesia, and the Portuguese colonies. Although they are sovereign and independent, their policies inevitably reflect influences from the countries under non-African governments. Of the five, Zambia is the least dependent on the non-African powers, while Lesotho is, in most respects, the most dependent.

Americans are so familiar with South Africa's discriminatory racial policy of apartheid that they tend to think of South Africa when Southern Africa is mentioned. As will be explained, however, Southern Africa is a geographic unit of considerable complexity.

Why Study Southern Africa?

It is important to study Southern Africa as a separate unit if a school is able to incorporate it into the curriculum for several reasons:

☐ The critical last remnants of the colonial conquest are in Southern Africa: Portuguese colonies in Angola and Mozambique, South African colonialism in Namibia, and alien settler domination in Rhodesia and South Africa, both of which practice a kind of internal colonialism in the pattern by which the White minorities rule the large African majorities.

Even though five Southern African countries have achieved political independence, European power still dominates their economic and political processes, and they are continually aware of the strength of European power in their geographic region.

☐ The treatment of Africans in their own homelands evinces one of the worst examples of racial injustice and oppression in the modern world. In an era in which Black peoples are struggling to achieve parity with the rest of the world, Southern Africa's racial injustices demand special recognition as one of the most serious human relations problems of our time.

☐ The UN continues to devote more of its attention to Southern Africa than any other region of the world. As a key member of the UN, the United States and its citizens must be thoroughly knowledgeable about Southern Africa and the grievous issues that it presents for UN debate and action.

☐ The independent nations of Africa constantly call Southern Africa's racial problem to the world's attention and the Organization of African Unity and other forums spend much of their energies on Southern African issues. Many people, in and out of Africa, feel that world peace is endangered by the continuing oppression of Africans in the southern part of the continent.

☐ Because some twelve percent of the American people are of African descent, and our own history has been so interwoven with problems of racial discrimination and efforts to achieve equality, Southern Africa is of special significance. It is an area in which the United States has a moral stake, because of the parallel between our problems and those of Southern Africa.

☐ United States trade and investment are larger in Southern Africa than in any other region of the continent; between one-third and one-half of the United States economic ties with Africa are with Southern Africa. Most of these are with the Republic of South Africa, where hundreds of large American firms maintain plants, major offices, subsidiaries, or investment interests.

Who Are the Southern Africans?

Southern Africa is generally known as the most racially complex region in Africa, with significant permanent populations of Africans, Europeans, Coloureds (of mixed race), and Asians (chiefly from India). Yet, as noted below, native Africans constitute more than eighty-five percent of the entire population and outnumber other groups by large proportions in every one of the ten southern African countries.

AFRICANS

Virtually all the Africans, who number approximately 44,000,000, speak Bantu languages and settled the region between 200 and 1500 A.D. In all essential respects they are similar to the peoples of Zaire, Cameroun, Kenya, Tanzania, Uganda, and other countries inhabited by Bantu-speaking peoples.

The original African inhabitants spoke various Khoisan languages and have been divided by European linguists into three major groups: Bushman, Hottentot, and Bergdama. Virtually all the latter two peoples are either extinct or have merged with Bantu or Coloured peoples to such an extent that their languages and cultures have disappeared; the Nama were the last large Hottentot group to survive into the twentieth century.

Of the Bushmen (whose own terms for themselves include Kung, Nusan, Xam, and Namib), most are today settled on European or African farms, although perhaps 10,000 to 15,000 still live nomadically in the great Namib and Kalahari deserts and the Okavango swamp of Botswana and Namibia. Their total surviving population is perhaps 60,000.

Bantu-speaking Africans moved into the Southern African region over a period of many centuries, gradually absorbing the nomadic Khoisan hunters and cattle herders. By the time of European contact in the sixteenth and seventeenth centuries, Southern Africa was inhabited by Bantu-speaking peoples except for isolated areas of little agricultural value and the southwestern tip of the continent, in what are now the western Cape Province of South Africa, southern Botswana, and southern Namibia.

EUROPEANS

Permanent European residents in Southern Africa number roughly 4,400,000, of whom there are three major groups: *Afrikaners*. Descendants of the original Dutch settlers of South Africa, together with smaller numbers of French Huguenots, Germans, Irish, Scots, and other Europeans. They number slightly over 2,000,000 and live almost entirely in South Africa.

British. Descendants of English-speaking settlers in various territories, numbering roughly 1,500,000 in South Africa, 250,000 in Rhodesia, 50,000 in Zambia, and less than 10,000 in each country of Malawi, Namibia, Botswana, Lesotho, and Swaziland.

Portuguese. Roughly 300,000 in Angola and 175,000 in Mozambique.

COLOUREDS

The great majority of the people called Coloureds are descendants of intermarriages between Dutch, Hottentot, African, and Malay people in the Cape of South Africa. Over the centuries they have become a separately identifiable group, who are largely European in culture and language (most speak Afrikaans). The Coloureds of South Africa number roughly 2,000,000, and there are small groups of African-European ancestry in most other countries of Southern Africa.

ASIANS

There are roughly 600,000 Indians in South Africa, mainly in Natal Province, who came as laborers to build railroads and work sugarcane plantations late in the nineteenth century. In addition, there are a few thousand in Mozambique, Malawi, Rhodesia, and Zambia.

Relations among these racial groups have never been smooth in Southern Africa. The Europeans have established a position of dominance and privilege over the other three groups by military conquest and continued rigorous control. Yet virtually all, despite tensions and embittered relations, agree that Southern Africa is a land in which all four groups have a legitimate place. Their permanence is rarely questioned, although the dominant position of Europeans is.

The Problems of Southern Africa

In one sense there is only one problem in Southern Africa—the tight control of the region by European settlers and Portuguese colonial power. Other problems abound, of course: underdeveloped economies, poor soils, poverty, social disorganization, lack of capital, unequal distribution of education and skills, disease, and rural–urban tensions. Yet these problems are so extensively affected by the disenfranchisement of Black by White that virtually all analysts agree that it is difficult to give them objective attention until the fundamental problem of racial inequality is solved.

The framework recommended for a study of Southern Africa and its problems is that of a combined topical and territorial approach that provides six points of focus: South Africa and its system of internal colonialism; the special status of Namibia as a South African dependency whose legal position is that of a United Nations Trust Territory; Rhodesia and its disputed ties with Britain; the Portuguese colonial position in Angola and Mozambique; the "captive" states of Botswana, Lesotho, Malawi, and Swaziland, whose economies depend heavily on that of South Africa; and the attempts by Zambia, with its mineral wealth, to break its historic dependence upon South Africa, Rhodesia, and the Portuguese territories.

SOUTH AFRICA:
APARTHEID AND INTERNAL COLONIALISM

Historical Sketch

Modern South Africa and its grievous race problems are best understood from a historical perspective; in a somewhat oversimplified sense, more than three centuries of South African history have been dominated by European conquest and the growth and consolidation of White power over Black. The following sketch is intended to provide an outline for the class to follow, not necessarily as a chronological approach, but as an effort to recognize the more significant events and forces in this history.

Before about 500 A.D. the only known inhabitants were the Khoisan peoples, who were nomadic hunters and herders of cattle.

After about 500 A.D. the Bantu-speaking peoples slowly settled the more northerly parts of the country, usually with little harsh conflict with the Khoisans. The Bantu-speaking peoples depended upon grain farming and cattle herding, and there was ample land for both peoples. By 1550 the Bantu-speaking peoples had moved as far south as the eastern Cape and north-central Botswana; the lands to their south and west were occupied by the Khoisans.

In 1652 the first party of Dutch colonists landed at Cape Town; they had been sent to establish a re-victualing station for Dutch ships plying between Asia and Europe. Despite opposition from the Dutch East India Company, individuals and small groups soon moved inland to settle as cattle farmers. Though the rate of growth was slow for the next century, it was inexorable, and by the late eighteenth century Dutch farmers (Boers) had occupied perhaps a third of what is now the Cape Province, seizing land from the Hottentot cattlemen as they expanded and developing their own way of life independent of close contact with the Dutch homeland.

In 1795 British naval forces occupied Cape Town during the Napoleonic War, returned it a few years later to Holland, then reclaimed it permanently in 1806 with the renewal of war. In 1820 the first large group of British settlers (5,000) landed at Port Elizabeth, in the eastern Cape, and began to settle land belonging to the Xhosa peoples.

Even earlier, in 1779, the first Kaffir War, or war between European settlers and Xhosa-speaking peoples, had resulted from disputes over land and cattle; by this time Boer farmers had settled along the western borders of Xhosaland. These wars continued intermittently for nearly a century (1789, 1799, 1812, 1818, 1834, 1846, 1850, and 1877), each time ending with the seizure of additional Xhosa land by the victorious Europeans. By the 1840s wars broke out with other African peoples farther north and continued until the beginning of the twentieth century.

The Boer farmers, irked by British restrictions in the Cape and especially by the abolition of slavery, began their Great Trek to the north in 1836. In 1852 their Transvaal Republic was internationally recognized, as was the Orange Free State in 1854. They had proclaimed a Natal Republic in 1836, but it was annexed by Britain in 1843.

Copper mining began in 1852, diamonds were discovered at Kimberley in 1867, and gold was found on the Witwatersrand in 1886, when Johannesburg was founded. British and other European investors, engineers, workers, and adventurers began settling the mining areas of the Orange Free State and Transvaal.

In 1899, following decades of conflict and tension between Britain and the Boer Republics, the Anglo-Boer War broke out; it ended with British victory and occupation in 1902.

In 1910 the modern Union of South Africa was founded, composed of the two British provinces (Cape and Natal) and the two Boer states (Orange Free State and Transvaal). It was a completely self-governing dominion within the British Commonwealth, similar to Australia, Canada, and New Zealand today.

The South African government was dominated by a coalition of British and Cape Boers from 1910 until 1948, except for a brief period of Afrikaner influence in the 1920s. In 1948 the National Party, based on Afrikaner votes, came to power on a platform of reassertion of the Afrikaans language and culture and White supremacy.

The National Party introduced the policy of apartheid, or racial separation, as a more comprehensive system than the pattern of segregation that had hitherto existed. During the 1950s the policy came to be called "separate development," emphasizing the possibility of African development in their own homelands and continuing European dominance in the White areas. By this time eighty-seven percent of the land of South Africa was in White hands and only thirteen percent in African hands. The White lands included the best agricultural regions; the African areas were seriously eroded, depleted, and overcrowded. More than forty percent of the African population lived in urban areas classified as White, while more than twenty-five percent lived on European farms. Only a third of the total African people lived in areas classified as "homelands."

Apartheid and Separate Development

Ever since the Dutch landed at Cape Town in 1652, segregation between White and Black has been practiced in South Africa, although some areas, such as that around Cape Town itself, have tended to be slightly less rigid than others. In homes, schools, churches, recreation, government, and employment the races have been kept apart by White insistence, with or without legal segregation ordinances. Segregation was developed to safeguard the racial, social, political, and economic dominance of Whites, who claimed that they achieved their affluence and highly developed society through the hard work and talent of themselves and their ancestors; they decry the role played by Africans, despite the fact that virtually all the labor has been performed by Black workers.

In the evolution of their society of privilege, South Africa's Whites have created a national myth (as do all nations), which overemphasizes their achievements and underemphasizes that of the Africans. A part of the myth, totally contrary to historical and archaeological evidence, is that Africans were not living in South Africa when Whites first arrived and that the two groups are both immigrants who have struggled to settle the country. Another part of the myth holds that Africans were (and largely still are) extremely primitive; phrases frequently used are "one step out of the trees," "two thousand years behind," and "still in the Stone Age." This belief ignores the considerable technological, artistic, intellectual, and political achievements made by Bantu-speaking peoples throughout their history, as well as their rapid acquisition of Western skills and abilities when allowed access to schools and jobs.

South African White society is indeed affluent and highly developed, fully comparable to those of Europe and North America: the universities are excellent, internationally recognized research is carried on, the country is virtually self-sufficient in industrial and manufactured products, and the White standard of living is very high.

Africans have been allowed little participation in the extensive development of South Africa: incomes average perhaps one tenth that of the Whites, few Africans can attend schools after the first two or three years, and most well paid jobs are either legally or *de facto* restricted to Whites. Yet Africans have largely abandoned their traditional way of life and are almost entirely dependent on the national economy for their livelihoods. For many decades they have moved into the cities (where they have long lived in townships on the fringes of the White areas), seeking work and improved opportunities. It is the consensus of the African people, most foreign observers, and many White South Africans that Africans long ago passed a point of no return in identifying their development with that of industrialized South Africa, so that the future of the country will inevitably require full African participation in economic and political affairs.

South Africa is a wealthy country if only the White population is considered; it is a poor country if the Blacks are considered. When both are considered together, it is clear that Black advancement would mean a lessening of White privilege and affluence, at least in the short run.

Apartheid and its successor, separate development, were created by Whites to insure that White power protects itself against future threat from Black advancement. The policy includes a number of features:

☐ Powerful control by the central government (Parliament and the administration) of all public affairs, and especially of the African community.

☐ A large, well organized, and efficient police and army to guard against subversion, effective political opposition, and threats to the status quo.

☐ An intricate, complex system of laws designed to prevent political change and African participation in national political or social affairs. Present laws empower the government to detain citizens without charge or trial, if they are believed to be potentially troublesome, and to imprison citizens (White or Black) for a variety of offenses that would seem to threaten the status quo.

☐ Disenfranchisement of Africans, so that they are prohibited from voting, holding office, or engaging in any political activity.

☐ Careful identification of all citizens according to their racial origin, and laws that prevent any social mixing or intermarriage between the various racial groups.

☐ Official decrees that give Africans few legal rights in non-African areas; outside the "homelands," the thirteen percent of the country set aside for African residence, all Africans are considered to be temporary visitors in White areas. They are permitted there only when they have bona fide jobs and permits to work, which must be periodically renewed.

☐ Development of a semblance of African political life in the homelands. Theoretically the homelands may one day become fully self-governing and economically developed states, although to date (the first, the Transkei, was officially established in 1963) there has been little economic development, little agricultural improvement, and no real power allowed African voters. The Territorial Assemblies that govern the several homelands have very limited powers, and the majority of their members are appointed by the South African government. Critics charge that the government has no sincere intention of allowing any real development within these African areas but is instead trying to build a facade of African development that will, in reality, insure that appointed African chiefs keep their people docile. According to this view, the separate development of the African areas is a sham whose real object is to maintain them indefinitely as reservoirs of cheap labor for the South African economy and legitimize the policy of complete disenfranchisement of Africans outside the homelands.

☐ An attitude of paternalistic colonialism by the Europeans toward the Africans. In many ways the African population (though it outnumbers the European four to one) is regarded as a conquered colonial population, and the Department of Bantu Administration functions like a powerful colonial government, ruling both directly and through powerless African tools.

South Africa and the World

Virtually no country in the world has come forward to defend South Africa's unique, harsh, exploitative race policies, yet many countries maintain friendly diplomatic and economic relations with it. Many free African nations have for years argued for intervention by the UN or the world's great powers, and apartheid has been officially denounced in the UN and by many governments (including that of the United States). Apart from an arms embargo, however, the great powers have refused to take positive action to try to induce change in South Africa. Even the arms embargo is feeble, since many nations have defied it, and South Africa has developed the ability to manufacture virtually all its military needs.

Study Suggestions

The reasons American students study South Africa (set forth above) focus on the moral and human implications of its racial system and the challenges they pose to Americans, as individuals and as citizens concerned with the foreign policy of their government. It is recommended, therefore, that the teacher devote ample time to study and discussion of the moral implications, African reactions, actions and debates within the UN, and the forces at work within the United States. The above historical and descriptive outlines are important for understanding what exists in South Africa and what created it, but are not intended as a substitute for this moral-contemporary focus. Below are a number of points for student investigation and discussion:

☐ What is the current United States policy toward South Africa? Pattern of trade, investment, and business relations? What forces operate in the United States that favor a stronger anti-South African position and a stronger pro-South African position? To what extent can American (or other foreign) actions influence developments within South Africa?

☐ What positions do the United Nations General Assembly, Security Council, and specialized agencies take on South Africa's internal policies? Why are more positive actions not taken? Under what circumstances might the UN play a stronger role? What might its effectiveness be?

☐ Which non-African countries tend to maintain the friendliest relations with South Africa, and for what reasons? Which are most critical of South Africa?

☐ Why do most African nations adopt a strong policy condemning South Africa's internal affairs? Why do some favor dialogue and closer economic ties with South Africa? To what extent can free African states influence affairs within South Africa or the outside world about South Africa?

☐ What are the moral implications of apartheid and separate development for an American? Do we have a right or a duty to attempt to change the internal condition of such a country? What about the frequent White South African comment that Americans have no right to comment on their problems since we have not solved our own race problems?

NAMIBIA: COLONY OR TRUST TERRITORY?

Called South-West Africa from the late nineteenth century until recently, Namibia has been renamed by the UN, in recognition of the claims of its African liberation leaders, and is the subject of extensive disputes between the UN and South Africa.

Germany seized South-West Africa in 1884 and held it until World War I, when South African troops defeated its German defenders. Under the League of Nations, South Africa administered the territory as a mandated territory but gradually deepened the ties between South-West Africa and the South African administration. By the 1940s South-West Africa was virtually a fifth province of the Union.

Under the UN, South Africa, a charter member, argued that her international responsibility for South-West Africa did not carry over to the UN trust system and thus South Africa had no obligation to prepare the people for independence or report to the UN on its administration. After years of litigation and debate, the UN General Assembly and the International Court ruled against South Africa, and a UN Committee for Namibia was appointed. To date the situation is still in dispute, and South Africa is applying its separate development policy in Namibia despite outside criticism.

There is no large body of European settlers in Namibia; roughly 80,000 Germans and South Africans live there among an African population in excess of 600,000. Only a few areas, mainly around the city of Windhoek in the central region, are fertile; most of the land is desert or arid grasslands, barely capable of sustaining cattle, sheep, and goats. Considerable mineral wealth, including diamonds, has been located and exploited.

As in South Africa, African political activity is forbidden, and Africans have no franchise. Under the separate development program a limited authority has been delegated to tribal groups in designated homelands, especially in Ovamboland in the north, but South African administrators retain control of all important areas of life.

The critical issue setting Namibia apart from South Africa is its different status. It is clearly a colony, whose nature is defined by the UN as that of a trust territory whose people should be prepared for full independence as expeditiously as possible. Since South Africa disputes this UN position, there is a stalemate, which seems likely to be broken only by forceful UN action. Few of the great powers, however, have so far been willing to agree to such action by the UN.

RHODESIA: THE INDEPENDENT BRITISH COLONY

Rhodesia, a populous country composed of nearly 5,000,000 Bantu-speaking Africans and some 250,000 Whites, chiefly of British descent, has a status even more enigmatic than that of Namibia. It is technically a British colony where Whites were granted self-government but not independence in 1923; in 1965, however, it declared itself fully sovereign and independent, but no country in the world has yet recognized its action. In 1966 Britain persuaded the UN to undertake an economic sanctions program designed to cripple the Rhodesian economy and force the country to capitulate to

British legal control; the sanctions have not produced this result, and the stalemate continues.

In 1972 Britain and Rhodesia reached an accord under which Rhodesian independence would be recognized if Africans were allowed gradual advancement toward full enfranchisement, if the majority of people in the country agreed to the settlement, and if there were constitutional safeguards against future change that might retard African progress. When a British commission traveled through the country seeking popular reactions, it found that Africans almost unanimously rejected the agreement. Their view is that their progress cannot be guaranteed unless they have more power and there is some outside supervision. They argue that the Whites are insincere in their promise of ultimate African participation in government on an equal basis. In the face of such determined African opinion, Britain had to renounce the agreement.

Africans in Rhodesia are not as fully disenfranchised as in South Africa and Namibia; a few thousand have the qualifications to vote, and there are African members of parliament (about one quarter of the total). But the more vocal African political parties have been outlawed and their leaders detained, imprisoned, or exiled. Those Africans in parliament are considered mild in their political leanings, and their popularity among the African people is questionable.

Whites in Rhodesia maintain a high standard of living, but the country is not wealthy. Much of its land is arid or of low fertility, and the Europeans have occupied most of the better farm lands. Mineral wealth is considerable, although modest when compared to that of South Africa or Zambia. As in South Africa, Whites would have to give up their present position of economic, political, and social privilege if Africans are to share in the country's wealth and future development, and few Whites are believed willing to do so. Yet the fact that there are so few Whites and so many Africans would indicate that sooner or later Rhodesia must become an African-ruled nation, despite White opposition. With African political expression tightly controlled, there has been a measure of conflict and guerilla activity based in surrounding free African nations, but the Rhodesian police and military seem to have maintained control without serious challenge.

Of special interest to Americans is the fact that the United States firmly supported the British-UN sanctions efforts until 1972 when the Senate voted to remove chrome (mined in Rhodesia by American companies) and several other items from the United States list of sanctioned goods. By this action the United States became one of the only countries in the UN to violate the sanctions program.

PORTUGUESE COLONIES

The Portuguese were the first Europeans to establish contact with Africa in the modern era and are the last to retain large colonies: Angola, Mozambique, and Portuguese Guinea, or Guinea (Bissau). Although Portugal has maintained a foothold in all three from the sixteenth century, it was not until the general European scramble for African territory late in the nineteenth century that it moved to extend its control. Portugal has long argued that these territories are not colonies or possessions but legal overseas provinces of Portugal; the Africans in the three territories, like most non-Portuguese observers, call them colonies.

There are significant Portuguese populations in Angola

(more than 300,000) and Mozambique (nearly 200,000), but few in Guinea. As is the case in South Africa and Rhodesia, using African labor, these settlers have built several thoroughly modern urban areas and have helped to develop some modern farms and industries. In general, however, the Portuguese colonies are poor and underdeveloped, due in part to the fact that Portugal itself is a small and poor country, ill equipped to undertake the development of its colonies.

Portugal has had a dictatorship form of government for nearly fifty years under the late Dr. Salazar and his successor, Mr. Caetano, and has consequently provided few democratic opportunities for either African or Portuguese subjects. Until 1961 Africans were not protected by Portuguese law (to the extent that it protected any citizens) unless they met certain qualifications of "assimilation," which then classified them legally as Portuguese citizens. Today, though their legal status has been changed, Africans still do not have the right to vote or to play any real role in Portuguese political affairs.

In 1960 military resistance to Portuguese rule began in Angola and Guinea, and in 1963 in Mozambique. African liberation forces control roughly half of Guinea, but their struggles in Angola and Mozambique have been less successful; they control the rural areas of at least two provinces in Mozambique and small areas of Angola, but no towns. Their war has made little headway in the past several years, partly because Portugal maintains large forces to combat them in both territories: 60,000 in Angola and 40,000 in Mozambique. Liberation movements from all the colonies maintain offices in exile but are able to operate only in a clandestine fashion inside the Portuguese-held areas.

A special item of importance to Americans is the fact that the United States continues to regard Portugal as an ally, especially in the context of NATO, and pays considerable sums of money for the use of Portugal's Azores Islands as air bases. African liberation leaders claim that American arms and ammunition flow from the United States to Portugal through NATO channels and are used to kill Africans; they argue that American military and financial support allows Portugal to continue allocating funds to the African wars that it could not otherwise afford. Evidence of oil deposits, especially in Angola, has attracted American oil investments and engineers, and African leaders protest this as economic support of Portuguese colonialism.

THE "CAPTIVE" NATIONS: BOTSWANA, LESOTHO, MALAWI, AND SWAZILAND

Although sovereign nations, these four countries are heavily dependent upon South Africa economically. Botswana, Lesotho, and Swaziland use South African currency and belong to a South African customs union; all three share long borders with and are virtually surrounded by South Africa. From each country, particularly Lesotho and Malawi, tens of thousands of men go to work each year in the South African mines. Without these jobs both countries would experience severe financial problems and massive unemployment.

Although the leaders and people of all four countries have indicated that they would prefer not to have such close ties with South Africa (all four forbid any kind of racial discrimination within their own borders), only Botswana seems, at present, to have some conceivable alternative—it has recently begun to produce copper and zinc from rich deposits. Of the four, only Malawi has borders with independent African nations, except for a tiny strip of a few hundred yards where Botswana and Zambia meet. All four are heavily dependent on South African manufactured goods, capital, skills, and communications facilities.

In American circles that follow African affairs there are two opposing views on the American role regarding the "captive" nations. One view argues that they are small and unimportant and so impoverished that the United States can do nothing to help them. The other view argues that United States government and private groups should provide special recognition and help for all four, in an effort to demonstrate that Africans can build sound nations, with reasonable help, even within the shadow of South Africa's apartheid system.

ZAMBIA: THE EFFORT TO BREAK FREE

Zambia, a relatively large country (4,500,000 population) with a substantial income from its huge copper mines, has for many years also been tied to the South African economy —buying South African goods, sending labor to South Africa's mines, and depending on South African skills and capital. But its dependence has been less than that of the four other independent states, and its geographical position is different. It has extensive borders with Zaire, Tanzania, Rhodesia, and Malawi, and it has maintained close communication with independent Africa, regarding Tanzania as a special ally. Its copper has traditionally been shipped to world markets via Rhodesian Railways (jointly owned, in the past, by Zambia and Rhodesia) through Mozambique or through Angola to the Atlantic. It has had no railroad links with Zaire or Tanzania to the sea.

With its strongly anti-apartheid views and its copper revenues, Zambia has followed a deliberate policy of reducing its ties with South Africa, Rhodesia, and the Portuguese areas and of strengthening its ties with Botswana, Tanzania, and Zaire. Much of its copper now travels by road to Dar es Salaam, Tanzania, and the Chinese are building the long and expensive Tan-Zam railway that will link Zambia railways with the sea at Dar es Salaam. It has tried to develop its own manufacturing industries where possible and to import goods through East Africa, to reduce its dependence on South African and Rhodesian products.

Zambia's efforts to break free from dependence on European settler governments and economies have met with considerable success but have been costly. Goods have been more expensive, funds have had to be spent on developing economic links to the north, and lower copper profits have resulted from shipping through Tanzania. Some Zambians have questioned the cost of the effort, but it continues as a major national policy and seems likely to allow Zambia to break away almost completely from its White neighbors in Southern Africa.

Study Suggestions for Southern Africa

Earlier in the chapter reasons for studying Southern Africa were outlined, and specific suggestions were made for approaching the study of South Africa and its apartheid system. Although it is valid to spend somewhat more time on South Africa than any of the other countries or problems of

Southern Africa, teachers are urged to devote time to a general consideration of the entire region, so that students can appreciate the different but interrelated aspects of European domination in that part of the African continent.

The following suggestions for approaches may be used by the teacher for the class as a whole, for groups or task forces of students, or for individual student's research.

THE AFRICAN PERSPECTIVE

☐ What does it mean to be an African in a region where White power is either directing one's day-to day life or affecting, more indirectly, one's society?

☐ What kinds of jobs are available? How does one train for them? What do they pay, and what are the conditions of work and promotion? What are the working relations between Black and White in the same company or agency?

☐ What form does religious worship take? What does one pray for and seek in all-African churches?

☐ What kinds of Africans serve in administrative positions? What are their relations with the peoples whose lives they affect?

☐ What is it like to live in a crowded African area outside a large European city? How do the police behave? What crimes are most common? How stable is the life of the family?

☐ How do Africans regard the African nationalist organizations that seek full African rights but are proscribed and often directed from headquarters in exile? (A list of the more important nationalist parties and their addresses in New York or London is given in the materials section.)

THE WHITE PERSPECTIVE

□ What does it mean to be a member of the dominant community, living a privileged life in the midst of large numbers of poor Africans?
□ What are the patterns of European life—residence, jobs, political views, family life, education?
□ What are White attitudes toward non-Whites?
□ What beliefs are held about Africa as one's homeland and the legitimacy of the White presence?
□ What are the patterns of racial segregation, White attitudes about segregation, and political movements for and against stronger segregation?

THE UNITED NATIONS PERSPECTIVE

□ How does the United Nations deal with the problems of Southern Africa in the General Assembly, the Security Council, Unesco, and its other agencies?
□ What resolutions have been passed in the past five years?
□ What actions have been taken to induce change in favor of African advancement?
□ What forces operate in favor of UN resolutions and actions, and what in opposition?

AMERICAN POLICIES PERSPECTIVE

As an American, how well does one understand both the official United States government policy toward Southern African problems and the various influences that shape that policy?

What are the policies of: Church groups and liberal groups? Firms with investment or trade in Southern Africa? Conservative groups and prosegregation forces? Defense Department and security forces? Black leaders and organizations

PERSPECTIVE OF CHANGE FORCES

☐ What forces are at work, both within Southern Africa and elsewhere in the world, that influence change in the European and African positions?

☐ What are the effects of economic growth in White-ruled countries: more industries, more need for African skilled labor, more European immigration, increased or decreased world markets?

☐ What changes in attitudes are taking place among Europeans and Africans, due to education, internal tensions, prosperity or depression, religion, political leadership, external developments?

☐ What are the effects of actions by outside forces: statements and actions by free African nations, the United Nations, various great powers, international associations and groups, and investors?

☐ What about efforts of African liberation movements to induce change by clandestine political organization, guerilla activity, sabotage, labor actions, demonstrations, and passive resistance?

☐ What developments in the African-ruled nations of Southern Africa, such as Botswana, Malawi, and Zambia, might make them more prosperous and less dependent on the White-ruled countries?

Teaching Materials

The study of Southern Africa should be a very important priority in the American curriculum on Africa. When to initiate the study, how, and for what duration of time are questions that can only be answered at the local level by teachers keenly attuned to local conditions.

Southern Africa is a region of intense interracial struggle. Studying the area may produce a totally unlooked-for set of spontaneous reactions from students and, perhaps, members of the public. One teacher has recalled that even on the first day of studying Southern Africa his students began planning a series of demonstrations against the town's largest employer which had a branch plant in South Africa. Sections of the tax-paying community may not want to see public education funds used with these conceivable results.

Teaching about Southern Africa is a very sensitive matter but is a rewarding task. Educators must deal with racial-political themes and assess the policy of the present and previous national administrations that have failed to meet African-expressed needs and desires. When selecting curriculum materials, educators should exercise more than the normal concern for objective and multisided treatment of these topics. The emergence of moral issues and the need to take a personal position should be encouraged. As educators know, this is both exciting and potentially divisive.

The emerging political-racial confrontation in Southern Africa has had direct implications for the development of American curriculums. Organizations representing both sides of the struggle are already seeking to influence course content. Educators will find at their disposal a variety of new and unique materials for inclusion in courses at the secondary level. Materials that may be characterized as propaganda may be extremely valuable instructional devices by which to introduce divergent positions and values.

By securing Southern African curriculum materials from a wide variety of sources, educators may present a number of varied and antagonistic positions to their students. Such materials may be used in world history classes, courses in government, African studies curricula, and possibly in evaluating United States foreign policy toward Africa within the confines of a United States history course. Some materials may also be useful in literature studies. For a review of revolutionary literature sources, see *Reader's Guide to African Literature* edited by H. Szell, Africana Publishing Company, 101 Fifth Ave., New York, N.Y. 10003. 1971 $4.95. pap.

GOVERNMENT SOURCES

Portugal, Rhodesia, and the Republic of South Africa maintain political and diplomatic representation in the United States, but only South Africa is making concerted efforts to influence American curricula.

The Portuguese, who consider Angola, Mozambique and Guinea as "overseas provinces," maintain a studied silence and have not specifically produced materials that seek to justify their position in Africa. Write to the following for general materials: Consulate General of Portugal, 640 Fifth Ave., New York, N.Y. 10019.

The Rhodesian regime maintains a political agent in Washington, D.C. He is registered as such with the Department of Justice. A tourist board function is also being continued. While the Rhodesian regime does seek to cultivate people and policies friendly toward its position, to date there has been no attempt to produce materials for American school curricula.

Tourist materials are available from: Rhodesian National Tourist Board, 545 Fifth Ave., New York, N.Y. 10019

The Republic of South Africa, through its Information Service, is deeply committed to influencing American curriculum development in favor of South and South-West Africa (Namibia). By writing to the Information Service, 645 Madison Ave., New York, N.Y. 10022, teachers may obtain weekly reviews of *South African News,* a monthly magazine, and a wide range of special booklets on such topics as Bantu education and medical care developments. All of these materials are available in mass quantity and are registered with the United States Department of Justice.

In recent years the South African government has attempted to influence American curriculum through a conduit arrangement with Audio-Visual Associates, a Division of Bear Films, Incorporated. By writing to Bear Films, 805 Smith St., Baldwin, N.Y. 11510, a teacher can secure free filmstrips, teaching handbooks, student materials, and attractive, colorful wall charts. These materials are South African government-produced and are registered with the United States Department of Justice. Recently Bear Films has been soliciting feedback from educators through a postage-paid postcard that solicits information and reaction concerning the free materials. This information is passed on to the South African government for consideration in the preparation of new materials.

The South African government also conduits its free films through Association Films, 600 Grand Ave., Ridgefield, N.J. 07657, and its regional film centers.

AMERICAN SOURCES

The first major American commercial curriculum package on Southern Africa was produced by Imperial Productions, Inc., Dept. AFC, Box 548, Kankakee, Ill. 60901. The 1969 kit consists of six tapes and filmstrips. Production of parts of the material required access to areas closed to tourists, and the producers extend appreciative thanks to the governments of Rhodesia and the Republic of South Africa for their assistance. As the kit is an American product, the materials are not registered with the Department of Justice. Very special care should be taken in any use of this kit. A teacher's guide is included. Total cost is $81.

In 1972, as part of a larger African studies project, Imperial produced a much expanded list of tapes and slides on Southern Africa. Angola and Mozambique were included, in addition to earlier efforts on Rhodesia (Zimbabwe), Namibia, and South Africa.

Tapes and coordinating slide sets present an extremely wide variety of themes. Each tape costs $9, and each slide set contains from four to thirty slides. Regardless of set, each slide costs fifty cents.

The items now available are:

	Tapes	Slide Sets
Mozambique	4	3
Rhodesia (Zimbabwe)	20	20
Republic of South Africa	96	47
Namibia	20	15
Angola	0	3

Reoccurring themes are tourism, internal economic development, development assistance being given to Africans by the White government, and racial diversity. Three of the

South African tapes present viewpoints opposed to current Nationalist government policies.

It should again be noted that many of the tapes required special government access permits to areas of Namibia, Rhodesia, and South Africa. This is a massive collection of materials that will require careful attention and sifting before incorporating them into any Southern African unit. When balanced by other materials reflecting the opposite point of view, however, many parts of the collection can have useful classroom applications.

For materials from organizations seeking to alter current conditions in Southern Africa, see the fall 1972 Southern Africa issue of *INTERCOM,* available for $1.50 from the African-American Institute, 866 United Nations Plaza, Room 505, New York, N.Y. 10017. The issue contains: an essay on Southern Africa by John Marcum, a political scientist specializing in Portuguese Africa, lesson plans for teaching about Southern Africa by Evelyn Jones Rich (co-author with Immanuel Wallerstein of *Africa: Tradition and Change,* Random House), resource guide to films and print materials, and materials available from many American organizations seeking to inform and change American involvement in Southern Africa. Highly recommended.

A new service to educators is called Project Dialogue. It offers speakers on various South African topics, supplemented by audio-visual presentations. There is no cost for the host institution. Project Dialogue was created by the Student Advisory Committee on International Affairs and the Carnegie Endowment for International Peace. The headquarters address is Suite 503, 1717 Massachusetts Ave., N.W., Washington, D.C. 20036. Regional offices are also maintained.

BRITISH SOURCES

With a little extra effort and patience, useful Southern African materials can be obtained from the following British sources:

The Africa Bureau, 48 Grafton Way, London W1, publishes *Africa Digest* six times a year. This contains an up-to-date summary of news from all over Africa with particularly good coverage of the South. There are also specialist pamphlets for sale, and *X-Ray* is a monthly bulletin providing factual information that has not been widely reported in Britain. It covers current affairs in Southern Africa.

African National Congress of South Africa, 49 Rathbone St., London W1. This is the office of the South African liberation movements in Britain, and it produces a monthly journal *Sechaba* as well as a small selection of pamphlets, e.g., *The African National Congress of South Africa—A Short History, Forward to Freedom—The Strategy, Tactics and Programme of the African National Congress*. The journal costs £1.50 (about $3.75).

Amnesty International, Turnagain Lane, 37 Farrington St., London EC4. Amnesty works for the release of prisoners of conscience all over the world, including Southern Africa, and tries to help their families in practical ways where possible. Each autumn a list of banned persons is made available to whom Christmas cards can be sent.

The Anti-Apartheid Movement, 89 Charlotte St., London W1. It produces *Anti-Apartheid News* every month, plus posters, pamphlets, and lists of companies involved in Southern Africa. There is also an education kit designed especially for schools.

The International Defence and Aid Fund, Christian Action, 2 Amen Court, London EC4. The Fund seeks to help those arrested in South Africa for political activities and supports their families while the breadwinners are imprisoned. It is banned in South Africa, and the Dean of Johannesburg was sentenced partly on the accusation that he helped to distribute money from it. It also produces some pamphlets on South Africa and conditions there.

RESOURCES FOR TEACHING ABOUT ZAMBIA

Although Southern Africa is a politically and economically integrated region, Zambia is recommended for educators interested in studying one nation within the area. Zambia is the largest and most important of the five landlocked, independent African states.

Basic References for Teachers

The High Price of Principles, Richard Hall. A sympathetic and first-hand account of recent political development in Southern Africa by former editor of *Times of Zambia.* Africana Publishing Company, 101 Fifth Ave., New York, N.Y. 10003. 1969. $7.50.

History of Central Africa, Louis Gann. General survey written from a European perspective with emphasis on colonial policies and economic development. Includes Malawi and Rhodesia. Prentice-Hall, Englewood Cliffs, N.J. 07632. 1971. $5.75.

A Short History of Zambia, rev. ed. Brian Fagan. Brief introduction with special emphasis on pre-twentieth century developments. Oxford University Press, 200 Madison Ave., New York, N.Y. 10016. 1968. $2.75. pap.

Zambia in Maps. Graphic perspectives of a developing country. Highly recommended. Contains references to all aspects of Zambian society. Africana Publishing Company, 101 Fifth Ave., New York, N.Y. 10003. 1972. $15.

Zambian Kit. Copies of the Zambian youth magazine *ORBIT*, designed for Zambian students and printed in English, can provide American students a direct insight into Zambian society and youth culture. It is available in a packet that consists of the following: 35 copies of *ORBIT* (both color and black and white), large picture of Zambian President, maps of Zambia, list of Zambian teaching resources, facts and data about Zambia from the Zambian government and banks, and Zambian government magazine Z. This will offer teachers and students both classroom materials and teacher references. Most important is that this curriculum effort is one of the few designed to introduce the Southern African region. African-American Institute, School Services Division, 866 United Nations Plaza, New York, N.Y. 10017. $9.95.

Economic and Population Data

Information Service, Population Reference Bureau, Inc.. 1755 Massachusetts Ave., N.W., Washington, D.C. 20036.

Monthly Economic Review, Standard Bank, 2 Wall Street, New York, N.Y. 10005.

Monthly Economic Survey, Barclays Bank D.C.O., 49th St. & Park Ave., New York, N.Y. 10017.

Newspapers

Times of Zambia, Box 394, Lusaka, Zambia.
Zambia Mail, Box 1421, Lusaka, Zambia.
  Write for subscription information.

Films and Filmstrips

Boy of Central Africa, 13½ min, color, 1968. Bailey Film
  Associates. $165, sale; $8, rental. Story of a young Zambian woodcarver's work in his village. Film may be used
  to supplement themes of rural to urban migration in
  search of opportunity and possible means by which
  rural areas may be developed.
Families of Modern Africa, color, 1970. Society for Visual
  Education. $26.50. Set of three filmstrips-records
  created for grades 5–8. One filmstrip concerns a family
  living in a copperbelt town. Others focus on Liberia and
  the Ivory Coast.

Government Information

Zambian Mission to the United Nations, 150 East 58th St.,
  New York, N.Y. 10022. Att: Public Affairs Officer.
Zambian National Tourist Bureau, 964 Third Ave., New
  York, N.Y. 10017.

9 Guidelines for selecting curriculum materials

Selecting materials is a complex process involving an analysis of available funds, student interests, personal values, departmental objectives, and available resources.

As world society changes and we learn more about the process of learning, curriculum materials are constantly being revised and replaced. Prices change constantly, usually upward. The film you wanted last year may no longer be available. New companies or curriculum projects will create new materials for your review. An understanding and use of guidelines for selection can help educators keep up with changing materials and developments.

As new items become available, keep in mind the research study completed by Dr. Barry Beyer and Dr. Perry Hicks and published in *Africa South of the Sahara: A Curriculum and Resource Guide*. (T. Y. Crowell, 201 Park Ave. South, New York, N.Y. 10001. 1969. $3.95.) Their work concluded that American students have distorted views of Africa and that between the seventh and tenth grades they are *learning much misinformation and learning it well*. This curriculum guide is highly recommended. You might also want to try out in your own class the test instrument Beyer and

Hicks used. Students already have a body of information and concepts before they enter your classroom. One night of a recent Tarzan movie, replete with a former professional football player and Olympic decathlon winner on national TV is tough to counter the next morning.

American students will soon be able to see at their local theaters a new set of African images. The *New York Times,* March 6, 1973, reported that a sequel to *Super Fly* is being filmed in Senegal, West Africa. The third shaft film, *Shaft in Africa,* was recently completed in Ethiopia.

Curriculum planners should also read two articles in the September/October and November/December issues of *Africa Report.* Entitled "African Studies Depend on a New Black History" and "African Studies: The Assumptions May Be Wrong," they concern the research study of Dr. Raymond Gildes, a Black American educator concerned with the extent and means by which Black American children identify with Africa and Africans.

The research study was conducted in 1969 in three Harlem elementary schools using a data base of 282 students. These students were receiving an intensive program in African studies and the staff was especially trained for the course. Giles concluded that after the course the students did not develop positive attitudes toward Africa and did not assist the students in identifying with Africans. The students knew more about the continent but presumably their self-esteem was not enhanced. A complete analysis of this doctoral dissertation will soon be forthcoming from Praeger Publishers, Inc. Back copies of these highly recommended issues can be obtained from *Africa Report,* 866 United Nations Plaza, New York, N.Y. 10017. $1.50 each.

NCSS Curriculum Guidelines

In 1971 the National Council for the Social Studies published a series of social studies curriculum guidelines that were created to assist educators evaluate materials. These guidelines should be used in assessing the value and usefulness of African materials. Following is a summary statement of the major guidelines:

1. A social studies program should be directly related to the concerns of the students.

2. A social studies program should deal with the real world.

3. A social studies program should draw from contemporary knowledge of man's experiences, cultures, and beliefs.

4. Objectives should be thoughtfully selected and clearly stated in ways to furnish direction to the program.

5. Learning activities should engage students directly and indirectly in the learning process.

6. Strategies of instruction and learning activities should rely on a broad range of learning resources.

7. A social studies program should facilitate the organization of experience.

8. Evaluation should be useful, systematic, comprehensive, and valid for the objectives of the program.

9. Social studies education should receive vigorous support as a vital and responsible part of the school program.

A detailed analysis of these major concepts is available in *Social Studies Curriculum Guidelines,* available from the National Council for the Social Studies, 1201 Sixteenth St., N.W., Washington, D.C. 20036 for $1.50. It is highly recommended for all teachers of social studies.

The March 1971 issue of *Social Education* devoted to Africa was jointly produced by the School Services Division of the African-American Institute and the NCSS. If your school doesn't have the issue, back copies are available from the African-American Institute, 866 United Nations Plaza, New York, N.Y. 10017. $1.50 prepaid.

Films and Filmstrips

Within the last five years the educational market has been inundated with African films and filmstrips. Many were created on the spur of the moment. Almost none have been formally tested in schools. Extreme caution is recommended before buying such materials. You can obtain useful materials if you know your needs. If you buy something you discover you can't use, you will probably be stuck with it for a few years.

Here are a few hints and criteria you might want to apply to the purchase of films and filmstrips on African geography. Note that these same criteria can and should be applied to the purchase of materials on Asia and South America. You may also teach these areas of the world in your courses.

THE BASIC QUESTIONS TO ASK

When was the film produced? Except for courses needing historical or comparative perspectives, the best rule is to consider post-1960 films. They should deal with contemporary themes from a non-colonial viewpoint.

Who produced the film? Films available from foreign

governments will convey government-sanctioned messages, which may or may not be adequate for your needs. United Nations' films reflect its priorities, as do films from airlines, which are seeking tourist business.

What audience is the target of the film? Certain films may contain described materials, but they may be oriented toward audiences different from yours.

Does the film *do the job for you?* African-Asian films can be continental surveys, regional surveys, single national studies, contemporary thematic studies, or social studies of institutions. What is it you want a film to introduce, or reinforce, or evaluate?

TECHNICAL POINTS FOR CONSIDERATION

☐ Is it expository, or does the film stimulate the teacher and students to think and reason as well as look and listen? How long is it?

☐ Is there a teacher's guide? Does the film try to do too much, i.e., overload information?

☐ Does the film link its content with other world areas or more universal problems? Is it applicable to situations, trends, and feelings in your own areas?

☐ Does it make an effort to give pronunciations or definitions? Does it stop its information transmission and occasionally review, more or less saying to itself, "I am a teaching instrument and not just a film"? Is this useful?

CONTENT CONSIDERATIONS

☐ If a survey, does the film show the diversity of humanity and environment in Africa? Is the contemporary and the urban stressed as well as the colonial period and the rural areas?

☐ Does the film focus on "exotica" or typical groups? Is it humanly sensitive, trying to place activities in their proper cultural perspective? Does the film portray Asians or Africans as they would portray themselves? Are the people personalized? Do they speak for themselves?

☐ Is the widest possible range of human roles and functions investigated? For instance, does a film on Kenya show only peasant farmers and no Kenyan lawyers, businessmen, TV producers, or artisans? Does a film on Nigeria show only urban workers and no farmers or fishermen?

Historical Overview

Before the 1960s African history was rarely studied in American schools. Usually whatever attention was given to the study of Africa occurred within the framework of European overseas expansion. World history largely examined the course of events in Western civilization. Other world areas were seldom included in social studies curriculum.

The history of African peoples was studied using European causal factors. Whenever European factors were not present the history of Europe was used as a model with which to compare and contrast African history. Isolated by geography, language, cultural arrogance, and occasionally by superior African political power, Europeans were largely unable or unwilling to objectively analyze and record the history of other peoples. It was also both expedient and politically useful to even deny the existence of a historical tradition in some parts of Africa. A people told that they had no record worth noting were psychologically colonized and rendered, in the colonial mind, intellectually sterile.

Until recently American textbooks reflected an Eurocentric view of African history. When educators evaluate texts or supplements in either print or audio-visual media, they should look out for these characteristics of an Eurocentric view of African history:

☐ The belief that little ever changed in Africa. Human existence was cyclical and lethargic as generations passed whole life styles on to succeeding generations.

☐ European colonialism shattered all aspects of an unchanging African life style. Rapid tumult resulted. This is known as the "big bang" theory.

☐ African history was a series of "contacts" initiated by Europeans. Books of this type focus on Graeco-Roman-African relations, the impact of Islam, the coming of the Portuguese, the Atlantic slave trade, the coming of the Dutch to the Cape of Good Hope, explorers, missionaries, or imperial partition.

☐ Inordinate attention given to the colonial impact, with recent European forms of control and cultural influence taking precedence over a longer continuum of history that should feature precolonial African history.

An African-centered view of history is beginning to appear in some materials. It is evidenced by such themes as:

☐ African peoples have determined the nature and direction of their own history.

☐ African societies, as with all peoples, have been changing and creative.

☐ There have been considerable intra-African exchanges of culture and ideas, largely unknown to an outside world.

☐ Many Africans have long been in contact with Asian

peoples and have developed historical links with them, again largely unknown to Europeans.

☐ African societies were diverse in nature and political forms of organization. Large political entities existed in multilingual kingdoms, as did small kinship groups.

☐ The colonial period was chiefly characterized by varying forms of African resistance and eventually by nationalistic struggles against the colonial powers.

In their individual search for balanced and reliable views of African history, American educators should choose materials using both Euro- and Afro-centric positions as a guide.

Contemporary Economic and Social Developments

Before actually selecting materials to teach about contemporary Africa, you should consider the following questions: What do you want your students to learn about Africa and Africans? What are the interests of your students? Where are the convergent points between your beliefs and their interests?

Only a few years ago, many educators were crying for materials that showed "modern" Africa. They wanted to counteract existing inaccurate information and stereotyped images. Many educators continue to seek such "modern" materials.

However, a counter-trend is now visible, especially in school systems with firmly established African studies programs. When shown a new magazine imported from Nigeria portraying a segment of urban youth culture, a teacher responded, "This stuff will turn them off. They don't want to see and read about Nigerian industry, city entertainment, and advertisements for locally produced consumer products. This is not the Africa they want to find." Material values and technological developments were defined by these students as "Western" and hence not African.

Most people would agree that materials reflecting the growth of new African cities and the changing life-styles of particular African cultures have to be balanced by examples portraying other aspects of African life.

Teachers continue to define and categorize Africans arbitrarily. It is undeniable and unavoidable. This is the nature of curriculum development. The essential point is to recognize the process, define objectives and priorities, and involve the students.

The Nigerian magazine mentioned above is available from the School Services Division, African-American Institute (866 United Nations Plaza, New York, N.Y. 10017, $9.95) in a kit consisting of thirty-five copies of *Teen and Twenty*, information and data on Nigeria, a West African bibliography, and pictures of West African presidents. It may turn your students off Africa and into a study of cultural diffusion and cultural values. You might discuss the Japanese businessman operating in Africa and whether or not he too is "Western." The salesman from Peking selling agricultural machinery would present another definition problem.

In an article in the *Washington Post* (June 26, 1972) columnist William Raspberry commented on the American and British impact in restaurants and night clubs he observed on his first day in Nairobi, Kenya. He was unable to find a Kenyan restaurant and was told that he really did not want to go to a restaurant where the average Nairobi Kenyan might eat. The music he heard was Isaac Hayes and Rare

Earth. The club's decor featured Jimi Hendrix and George Harrison. Mr. Raspberry noted that the Kenyans in these places seemed "somehow pasteurized and perhaps over-Anglicized." He was unable to find Black people having a good time and enjoying themselves. He wrote that on the following night he was determined to continue his search for Kenyans living as Kenyans.

An article in the *Louisville Courier-Journal* (April 30, 1972) by a former Nigerian diplomat stressed the need to avoid the creation of a new mythology about modern Africa. He noted that Afro-hairdos were not indigenous to the African continent and that slavery and the slave trade existed before the development of the West Indies plantation economy. These facts irritated some Americans. The author concluded that his countrymen were afraid to express certain facts about Africa, preferring to tell Americans what they wanted or expected to hear.

Different styles of life in Africa pose definitional and value questions for Americans. Some African intellectuals believe African culture is simply the way Africans live today. President Mobutu of Zaire (formerly Congo, Kinshasa), for example, has implemented an authenticity program in an effort to release Zaireans from feeling that they are caught between two cultures. According to the President, "We want him to feel at ease in his skin, freed from the complexes so that he can freely grasp all the attributes of the modern world, adopt them, assimilate them in harmony, and gently adapt them to his own culture." His concepts can form a rationale for informing American students about changing styles of life in contemporary Africa.

Choosing African curriculum materials requires the same evaluation used in any other selection process. A recent article in the *Elementary School Journal* (September, 1972) by M. F. Klein and L. I. Tyler outlined six essential steps:

1. Analyze the product's rationale
2. Assess the specifics of the intended objectives
3. Decide its appropriateness for students
4. Attempt to predict effectiveness
5. Is it practical for your conditions?
6. Do you have enough information to make a "buy" or "no sale" decision?

It may take considerable time to develop your curriculum of African study. For many educators, students, parents, and citizens, the study of Africa involves a different process from studying any other world region. It is something very special and linked to psychological and political realities in contemporary America.

Appendix:
Visual/Media Resources

University-Developed Curriculum

African Studies Handbook for Teachers, Part 1. Compiled
by Worcester, Massachusetts, Teacher Corps Project.
Introductory lessons on Africa for both elementary and
secondary classes developed by former Peace Corpsmen
with African experience; they are competency-based in
format and affective in purpose. Included is a bibliography of books and audio-visual materials about Africa.
Individual lessons and slide packages for African studies also available. Center for International Education,
School of Education, University of Massachusetts, Am-
herst, Mass. 01002. 1972. $2.50.

The Family of Man. A social studies program based on the
work of the University of Minnesota Project Social
Studies Curriculum. Detailed information is given on
page 57.

Project Africa. A secondary-level curriculum development
project based at Carnegie-Mellon University in Pittsburgh under the direction of Dr. Barry Beyer and Dr.
Perry Hicks. For details on Project Africa, curriculum
information, and consulting services contact Dr. Barry

Beyer, Department of History, Baker Hall, Carnegie-Mellon University, Schenley Park, Pittsburgh, Pa. 15213.

Major Commercial Sources

FILMS

☐ Association-Sterling, 660 Grand Ave., Ridgefield, N.J. 07659

☐ Bailey Film Associates, 2211 Michigan Ave., Santa Monica, Calif. 90404

☐ Carousel Films, 1501 Broadway, New York, N.Y. 10027

☐ Churchill Films, 662 North Robertson Blvd., Los Angeles, Calif. 60069

☐ Cokesbury Service Center, 1600 Queen Anne Rd., Teaneck, N.J. 07666

☐ Coronet Films, 65 E. South Water St., Chicago, Ill. 60601

☐ Crowell, Collier-Macmillan, 866 Third Ave., New York, N.Y. 10022

☐ Doubleday Multimedia, Doubleday and Co., Inc., Garden City, N.Y. 11530

☐ Encyclopaedia Britannica Educational Corp., 425 North Michigan Ave., Chicago, Ill. 60611

☐ Films Incorporated, 1144 Wilmette Ave., Wilmette, Ill. 60091

☐ Holt, Rinehart & Winston, 383 Madison Ave., New York, N.Y. 10017

☐ International Communication Films, 1371 Reynolds Ave., Santa Ana, Calif. 92705

☐ International Film Bureau, 332 South Michigan Ave., Chicago, Ill. 60604

☐ International Film Foundation, 475 Fifth Ave., Room 916, New York, N.Y. 10017

☐ Learning Corporation of America, 711 Fifth Ave., New York, N.Y. 10022

☐ McGraw-Hill Films Division, 1121 Sixth Ave., New York, N.Y. 10036

☐ N.B.C. Films, Rockefeller Plaza, New York, N.Y. 10019

☐ Sengal Productions, 625 West 42nd St., New York, N.Y. 10036

☐ Sterling Educational Films, 241 East 34th St., New York, N.Y. 10016

☐ Texture Films, Inc., 1600 Broadway, New York, N.Y. 10019

☐ Time-Life Films, Inc., 14 West 16th St., New York, N.Y. 10009

FILMSTRIPS

☐ Bailey Film Associates, 2211 Michigan Ave., Santa Monica, Calif. 90404

☐ Brady (Robert J.) Co. (subsidiary of Prentice-Hall, Inc.), 130 Que St., N.E., Washington, D.C. 20002

☐ Contemporary Media Inc., Box 58-H, Scarsdale, N.Y. 10583

☐ Coronet Films, Inc., 65 East South Water St., Chicago, Ill. 60601

☐ Crowell (Thomas Y.) Co., 201 Park Ave. South, New York, N.Y. 10003

☐ Crowell, Collier-Macmillan, 866 Third Ave., New York, N.Y. 10022

☐ Current Affairs Films, 527 Madison Ave., New York, N.Y. 10022

☐ Doubleday Multimedia, Doubleday and Co., Inc., Garden City, N.Y. 11530

☐ EMC Corporation, 130 East 6th St., St. Paul, Minn. 55101

☐ Encyclopaedia Britannica Education Corp., 18 East Post Rd., White Plains, N.Y. 10601

☐ Eye Gate House, Inc., 146-01 Archer Ave., Jamaica, N.Y. 11435

☐ Guidance Associates, Pleasantville, N.Y. 10570

☐ International Book Corp., 7300 Biscayne Blvd., Miami, Fla. 33138

☐ International Media, 144 Main St., Hackensack, N.J. 07601

☐ Imperial Film Company, P.O. Box 1007, Lakeland, Fla. 33803

☐ Imperial Productions, Inc., Kankakee, Ill. 60901

☐ McGraw-Hill Film Division, 1121 Sixth Ave., New York, N.Y. 10036

☐ Multi-Media Productions, 580 College Ave., Palo Alto, Calif. 94306

☐ Museum Extension Service, 83 Adams St., Bedford Hills, N.Y. 10507

☐ New York Times, Office for Educational Activities, 229 West 43rd St., New York, N.Y. 10036

☐ Schloat (Warren) Productions, Inc., 115 Tompkins Ave., Pleasantville, N.Y. 10570

☐ Scott Education Division, Holyoke, Mass. 01040

☐ Society for Visual Education, 1345 Diversey Parkway, Chicago, Ill. 60614

☐ Sterling Educational Films, 241 East 34th St., New York, N.Y. 10016

☐ Time-Life Films, Inc., 14 West 16th St., New York, N.Y. 10019

☐ Universal Films, Universal Education and Visual Arts, 221 Park Ave. South, New York, N.Y. 10003
☐ Westinghouse Learning Press, Film Division, 100 Park Ave., New York, N.Y. 10017

Film Rental Libraries

Many libraries have African collections. Generally, these are films. Only one print may be available. Films from public television are usually held in these libraries, as are films photographed by academic staff for research or teaching purposes. The following libraries have useful collections and merit your investigation.

ARIZONA

Arizona State University, Audio Visual Center, Tempe, Ariz. 85281
University of Arizona, Bureau of Audio Visual Services, Tucson, Ariz. 85721

CALIFORNIA

University of California, Extension Media Center, 2223 Fulton St., Berkeley, Calif. 94720
University of Southern California, Division of Cinema, Film Distribution Section, University Park, Los Angeles, Calif. 90007

COLORADO

Bureau of Audio Visual Instruction, Stadium Room 320, University of Colorado, Boulder, Colo. 80304

CONNECTICUT

University of Connecticut, Audio Visual Center, Storrs, Conn. 06268

FLORIDA

Florida State University, Media Services, Tallahassee, Fla. 32306

University of South Florida, Division of Educational Resources, 4202 Fowler Ave., Tampa, Fla. 33620

GEORGIA

University of Georgia, Film Library, Athens, Ga. 30601

IDAHO

University of Idaho, Audio Visual, Moscow, Id. 83843

ILLINOIS

Southern Illinois University, Audio Visual Aids Service, Carbondale, Ill. 61820

University of Illinois, Visual Aids Service, 704 South Sixth St., Champaign, Ill. 61920

INDIANA

Indiana University, Audio Visual Center, Bloomington, Ind. 47401

IOWA

State University of Iowa, Bureau of Audio Visual Instruction, Iowa City, Iowa 52240

KENTUCKY

University of Kentucky, Audio Visual Center, Lexington, Ky. 40506

MASSACHUSETTS

Boston University, Abraham Krasker Memorial Film Library, 765 Commonwealth Ave., Boston, Mass. 02215

MICHIGAN

Michigan State University, Instructional Media Center, East Lansing, Mich. 48823
University of Michigan, Audio Visual Education Center, 416 Fourth St., Ann Arbor, Mich. 48103

MINNESOTA

University of Minnesota, Dept. of Audio Visual Extension, 2037 University Ave., S.E., Minneapolis, Minn. 55455

MISSISSIPPI

University of Mississippi, Audio Visual Education, University, Miss. 38677

MISSOURI

University of Missouri, Audio Visual & Communications, 119 Whitten Hall, Columbia, Mo. 65201

NEBRASKA

University of Nebraska, Instructional Media Center, Lincoln, Neb. 58608

NEW HAMPSHIRE

University of New Hampshire, Audio Visual Center, Durham, N.H. 03824

NEW JERSEY

State Department of Education, Audio Visual Education, Trenton, N.J. 08625

State University of New York, Instructional Communication Center, Media Library, 22 Foster Annex, Buffalo, N.Y. 14214
Syracuse University, Rental Library, 1455 East Colvin St., Syracuse, N.Y. 13210
Yeshiva University, Audio Visual Center, 526 West 187th St., New York, N.Y. 10033

NORTH CAROLINA

University of North Carolina, Bureau of Audio Visual Education, Chapel Hill, N.C. 27514

OHIO

Kent State University, Audio Visual Services, 221 Education Building, Kent, Ohio 44240

OREGON

Oregon State University, Audio Visual Instruction, 133 Gill Coliseum University Campus, Corvallis, Ore. 97331

PENNSYLVANIA

Pennsylvania State University, Audio Visual Aids Library, University Park, Pa. 16802

TEXAS

University of Texas, Visual Instruction Bureau, Division of Extension, Austin, Tex. 78712

UTAH

Brigham Young University, Educational Media Services, 290 Herald R. Clark Building, Provo, Utah 84601
University of Utah, Educational Media Center, 207 Bennion Hall, Salt Lake City, Utah 84112

University of Vermont, Audio Visual Center, Burlington, Vt. 05401

WASHINGTON

Central Washington State College, Audio Visual Library, Ellensburg, Wash. 98926
University of Washington, Audio Visual Services, Booking Dept., Seattle, Wash. 98105
Washington State University, Audio Visual Center, Pullman, Wash. 99163

WISCONSIN

University of Wisconsin, Bureau of Audio Visual Instruction, 1312 West Johnston St., Madison, Wis. 53715

Free Films

Association-Sterling can be contacted at any of its regional offices for free films. *You will have to pay the return postage.* They have a few films on Africa from UNESCO and United States companies with investments in Africa. Order six months ahead to insure receipt of films.

2535 Cypress Ave., Hayward, Calif. 94544
2221 South Olive St., Los Angeles, Calif. 90007
324 Delaware Ave., Oakmont, Pa. 15139
8615 Directors Row, Dallas, Tex. 75247
5797 New Peachtree Rd., Atlanta, Ga. 30340
512 Burlington Ave., La Grange, Ill. 60525
484 King St., Littleton, Mass. 01460
600 Grand St., Ridgefield, N.J. 07857
915 N.W. 19th Ave., Portland, Ore. 97209

6420 West Lake St., Minneapolis, Minn. 55426
4980 Buchan St., Montreal, Quebec
333 Adelaide St.. W., Toronto 133, Ontario

Filmographies

African Studies Newsletter, vol. 5, no. 2, April 1972. Contains a twenty-eight page critical review of twenty-one films. Useful for senior high school teachers. Filmography is available from African Studies Association, 218 Shiffman Humanities Center, Brandeis University, Waltham, Mass. 02154

"Audio Visual Aids for African Studies." An essay by William G. Byrne in the *African Experience,* vol. III B, *Guide to Resources,* Chapter 5. Covers audio-visual resources for college introductory courses in African studies. Evaluates films thematically and includes useful listing of distributors. Northwestern University Press, 1735 Benson Ave., Evanston, Ill. 60201. 1971. $5. pap.

Film Catalog, 1966. Analysis of films on a country-by-country basis. Council of the African-American Institute, 866 United Nations Plaza, Room 505, New York, N.Y. 10017. $3.

A List of Films on Africa compiled by Claudia W. Moyne. Development Program, African Studies Center, Boston University, 10 Lexon St., Brookline, Mass. 02146. July 1966; revised July 1968. $2.50.

Teaching African Development with Film. N. Miller. Created for university-level courses. Contains analytical essay and extensive listing of films and distributors. American Universities Field Staff, 3 Lebanon St., Hanover, N.H. 03755.